IDIOSYNCRATIC DEALS BETWEEN EMPLOYEES AND ORGANIZATIONS

Idiosyncratic deals, or i-deals, are the individualized working arrangements negotiated by employees with the organizations for which they work. Such deals represent an emerging area of study into the effects they have on both parties, as well as co-workers and the wider working world. Do i-deals signify a further breakdown of collectivism within the workplace, or should they be seen as empowering to those employees able to find themselves the best deal? Is the growth of i-deals an inevitable response to the need for more flexible working relationships, or do they erode concepts of equality and fairness?

In this important new collection, i-deals are discussed from a comprehensive range of viewpoints. The book examines how i-deals alter the psychological relationship between employee and employer, as well as the notion of career development in an aging and technologically literate workforce. The issue of group relationships is also discussed, in relation to leadership theories, organizational justice and perceived fairness. Finally, the impact on organizational and individual effectiveness is assessed. Are i-deals a good thing for employers looking to maximize productivity within an organization? Do employees work more effectively and efficiently as a consequence of i-deals?

Very much a hot topic, this volume represents a key contribution in the area of i-deals from the most active researchers in the field. It will be important reading for all students of work and organizational psychology, human resource management and business management.

Matthijs Bal is a Reader at the School of Management, University of Bath, UK.

Denise M. Rousseau is H.J. Heinz II Professor of Organizational Behavior and Public Policy at Carnegie Mellon University, USA.

Current issues in work and organizational psychology
Series Editor: Arnold B. Bakker

Current Issues in Work and Organizational Psychology is a series of edited books that reflect the state-of-the-art areas of current and emerging interest in the psychological study of employees, workplaces and organizations.

Each volume is tightly focused on a particular topic and consists of seven to ten chapters contributed by international experts. The editors of individual volumes are leading figures in their areas and provide an introductory overview.

Example topics include: digital media at work, work and the family, workaholism, modern job design, positive occupational health and individualized deals.

Idiosyncratic Deals between Employees and Organizations: Conceptual issues, applications and the role of co-workers
Edited by Matthijs Bal and Denise Rousseau

A Day in the Life of a Happy Worker
Edited by Arnold B. Bakker and Kevin Daniels

The Psychology of Digital Media at Work
Edited by Daantje Derks and Arnold B. Bakker

New Frontiers in Work and Family Research
Edited by Joseph G. Grzywacz and Evangelia Demerouti

Time and Work, Volume 1: How time impacts individuals
Edited by Abbie J. Shipp and Yitzhak Fried

Time and Work, Volume 2: How time impacts groups, organizations and methodological choices
Edited by Abbie J. Shipp and Yitzhak Fried

Burnout at Work: A Psychological Perspective
Edited by Michael P. Leiter, Arnold B. Bakker, and Christina Maslach

Towards Inclusive Organizations: Determinants of successful diversity management at work
Edited by Sabine Otten, Karen Van Der Zee, and Marilynn Brewer

Well-being and Performance at Work: The role of context
Edited by Marc van Veldhoven and Riccardo Peccei

Employee Recruitment, Selection, and Assessment: Contemporary issues for theory and practice
Edited by Ioannis Nikolaou and Janneke K. Oostrom

IDIOSYNCRATIC DEALS BETWEEN EMPLOYEES AND ORGANIZATIONS

Conceptual issues, applications and the role of co-workers

Edited by
Matthijs Bal and Denise M. Rousseau

LONDON AND NEW YORK

First published 2016
by Routledge
2 Park Square, Milton Park, Abingdon, Oxon OX14 4RN

and by Routledge
711 Third Avenue, New York, NY 10017

Routledge is an imprint of the Taylor & Francis Group, an informa business

© 2016 Matthijs Bal and Denise M. Rousseau

The right of Matthijs Bal and Denise M. Rousseau to be identified as the authors of the editorial material, and of the authors for their individual chapters, has been asserted in accordance with sections 77 and 78 of the Copyright, Designs and Patents Act 1988.

All rights reserved. No part of this book may be reprinted or reproduced or utilised in any form or by any electronic, mechanical, or other means, now known or hereafter invented, including photocopying and recording, or in any information storage or retrieval system, without permission in writing from the publishers.

Trademark notice: Product or corporate names may be trademarks or registered trademarks, and are used only for identification and explanation without intent to infringe.

British Library Cataloguing-in-Publication Data
A catalogue record for this book is available from the British Library

Library of Congress Cataloging-in-Publication Data
Idiosyncratic deals between employees and organizations : conceptual issues, applications and the role of co-workers / edited by Matthijs Bal and Denise M. Rousseau. — 1 Edition.
    pages cm
 1. Industrial relations. 2. Negotiation. 3. Deals. 4. Individual bargaining. I. Bal, Matthijs, editor. II. Rousseau, Denise M., editor.
    HD6971.I35 2016
    331—dc23
    2015012123

ISBN: 978-1-848-72445-7 (hbk)
ISBN: 978-1-315-77149-6 (ebk)

Typeset in Bembo
by Apex CoVantage, LLC

Printed and bound by CPI Group (UK) Ltd, Croydon, CR0 4YY

CONTENTS

List of Contributors		*vii*
1	Introduction to idiosyncratic deals between employees and organizations: conceptual issues, applications and the role of co-workers *Matthijs Bal and Denise M. Rousseau*	1
2	Individualization of work arrangements: a contextualized perspective on the rise and use of i-deals *Matthijs Bal and Xander D. Lub*	9
3	I-deals in damaged relationships *Sylvie Guerrero and Kathleen Bentein*	24
4	Not so i-deal: a critical review of idiosyncratic deals theory and research *Neil Conway and Jacqueline Coyle-Shapiro*	36
5	An i-deal career: on the relationship between i-deals and career development *Aukje Nauta and Cristel van de Ven*	65
6	A strategic HRM perspective on i-deals *Brigitte Kroon, Charissa Freese, and René Schalk*	73
7	Idiosyncratic deals in the context of workgroups *Smriti Anand and Prajya Vidyarthi*	92

8 Equity versus need: how do coworkers judge
   the distributive fairness of i-deals?   107
   Elise Marescaux and Sophie De Winne

9 The future of i-deal research: an agenda   122
   Matthijs Bal and Denise M. Rousseau

Index   *131*

CONTRIBUTORS

Smriti Anand, Illinois Institute of Technology, United States

Matthijs Bal, University of Bath, United Kingdom

Kathleen Bentein, University of Quebec at Montreal, Canada

Neil Conway, Royal Holloway University of London, United Kingdom

Jacqueline Coyle-Shapiro, London School of Economics, United Kingdom

Sophie De Winne, KU Leuven, Belgium

Charissa Freese, Tilburg University, the Netherlands

Sylvie Guerrero, University of Quebec at Montreal, Canada

Brigitte Kroon, Tilburg University, the Netherlands

Xander D. Lub, Saxion University of Applied Sciences, the Netherlands

Elise Marescaux, KU Leuven, Belgium

Aukje Nauta, University of Amsterdam, the Netherlands

Denise M. Rousseau, Carnegie Mellon University, United States

René Schalk, Tilburg University, the Netherlands

Cristel van de Ven, Factor Vijf, the Netherlands

Prajya Vidyarthi, University of Texas at El Paso, United States

1
INTRODUCTION TO IDIOSYNCRATIC DEALS BETWEEN EMPLOYEES AND ORGANIZATIONS

Conceptual issues, applications and the role of co-workers

Matthijs Bal and Denise M. Rousseau[1]

Introduction

Individual agreements between employees and their organizations have become increasingly normalized in the contemporary labor market (Miner, 1987; Rousseau, 2001). Valuable employees negotiate special arrangements with their employers, in order to obtain desirable work arrangements, and organizations grant employees these inducements because they want to retain them for the organization or to motivate them in their work. Idiosyncratic deals (henceforth i-deals) are special conditions of employment negotiated between an individual worker and his or her employer (Rousseau, 2005). The rise of i-deals in organizations has been spurred by a number of societal trends, including the increased power of groups of employees who have valuable skills that organizations desire to attract or retain. Moreover, diversification of demands in the market has also impacted employment relationships (Kooij, Rousseau, & Bal, 2014). A growing number of organizations have introduced flexible work arrangements and customization of jobs in order to be able to motivate employees who are currently in the workplace. At the same time, new economic realities demand organizations to become more flexible and better able to rapidly adapt to changing circumstances in the market, through which more and more organizations try to build a more flexible workforce. Employees hence are also expected to be more flexible, proactive, and able to adapt to changing work conditions (Bal & Jansen, 2014; Grant & Parker, 2009). Furthermore, due to increased individualization of societies and the decreasing influence of trade unions, employees have the opportunity for more individualized employment relationships (Rousseau, 2005), but at the same time they also experience increased responsibility for their own careers and well-being. Hence, individualization has led to a growing number of employees negotiating individual agreements with their employers.

In scientific terms, these individual agreements have been researched in the context of idiosyncratic deals, or i-deals for short.

I-deals have been defined by Rousseau (2001, 2005; Rousseau, Ho, & Greenberg, 2006, p. 978) as "voluntary, personalized agreements of a nonstandard nature negotiated between individual employees and their employers regarding terms that benefit each party." According to Rousseau and colleagues (2006), there are a number of features that define i-deals and distinguish them from related constructs, such as preferential treatment or favoritism. First, i-deals are individually negotiated and can be initiated by both employee and organization, even though typically i-deals are initiated by the employee (Rousseau, 2005). Hence, individual employees negotiate with their organization a specific idiosyncratic arrangement. When employment arrangements are collectively negotiated, they become part of an HR system in an organization (or they are part of collective labor agreements or law) and available to every employee. For instance, there is a body of research on flexible work arrangements, such as teleworking and flexible work schedules, which are implemented by organizations in order to facilitate employees with greater flexibility (Allen, Johnson, Kiburz, & Shockley, 2013; Baltes, Briggs, Huff, Wright, & Neuman, 1999). These types of HR policies and practices ensure every employee the right to use a certain practice, and hence is no longer an i-deal.

I-deals are also heterogeneous, such that arrangements are negotiated that differ from the work conditions that other employees have (Rousseau et al., 2006). This heterogeneity may also indicate measurement issues, since every negotiated i-deal may be different and therefore difficult to measure for researchers. As noted, i-deals create heterogeneity among workers within the same organization and within the same work groups, and thus increased heterogeneity among workers in similar positions may create perceptions of unfairness, since some employees might be more successful in negotiating i-deals than others. Inequality among workers in the same departments or units may create challenges for organizations and managers to ensure organizational fairness, both in the outcomes employees negotiate as well as the procedures used by the organizations to come to decisions regarding i-deals (Greenberg, Roberge, Ho, & Rousseau, 2004). Furthermore, i-deals benefit both employee and organization. For employees, i-deals fulfill the need for customized work arrangements that may facilitate motivation, productivity or well-being, while at the same time, i-deals benefit employers because they may attract, retain or motivate valuable employees. Consequently, i-deals differ from favoritism, cronyism, nepotism and corruption, such that the basis of the agreement lies within legitimacy of shared values, while these other types of preferential treatment do not have such basis. When an i-deal is negotiated between an employee and the organization, the legitimacy of the deal should be notable in the public notification of the deal, such that acceptance by co-workers is obtained (Lai, Rousseau, & Chang, 2009). Finally, i-deals vary in scope – some employees may negotiate a single idiosyncratic deal, such as the possibility to vary working times during the workweek, while others may have a fully idiosyncratically negotiated position. The relative proportion of idiosyncratic features of a job may vary to a large degree among workers (Rousseau et al., 2006).

Since Rousseau's (2001, 2005) seminal publications on i-deals, an increasing number of studies have been devoted to the topic. The majority of these publications have focused on the antecedents and consequences of i-deals, such as who are likely to negotiate i-deals and how i-deals relate to outcomes such as commitment and employee performance (Hornung, Rousseau, & Glaser, 2008; Rousseau, Hornung, & Kim, 2009). Moreover, studies have been conducted in which measures of i-deals are developed and validated (Rosen, Slater, Chang, & Johnson, 2013). The majority of these studies have focused on employee perceptions of i-deals, through asking employees the types of i-deals they have negotiated with their employer. Two exceptions to this approach have been published by Hornung and colleagues (2009), who assessed among managers whether they had negotiated i-deals, and Lai and colleagues (2009), who investigated co-workers' reactions to negotiated i-deals. Apart from these two studies, all studies have focused on these employee perceptions of i-deals. It is notable that research on i-deals follows a similar development as research on psychological contracts (Rousseau, 1995), with a conceptual focus on the exchange relationship between employee and organization, while the vast majority of empirical research on the topic has been devoted to employee perceptions of this exchange, thereby ignoring the employer's view.

The theoretical underpinning of how i-deals operate in the workplace has primarily been found in social exchange theory (Blau, 1964) and, in particular, the norm of reciprocity (Gouldner, 1960). The employee and the employer engage in an exchange relationship, in which they exchange resources that are valuable to each party, such as services by the employee for financial rewards and development provided by the employer. I-deals form the basis of a further refinement of the exchange relationship, through which employee and organization agree over a personalized exchange of resources that matter to each party. When the organization grants the employee an i-deal, it expects the employee to reciprocate the favorable treatment through higher effort, motivation, or simply retention of the employee within the firm. As such, i-deals create a strengthening of the employment relationship. Research has shown that i-deals relate to positive outcomes (Anand, Vidyarthi, Liden, & Rousseau, 2010; Hornung et al., 2008; Rosen et al., 2013), and they may even contribute to the motivation to continue working beyond retirement (Bal, De Jong, Jansen, & Bakker, 2012). Hence, i-deals may constitute an important element in the employment relationship, through which organizations attract employees, motivate them in their jobs, and maintain employee motivation in the long run.

Other theoretical perspectives on i-deals have been founded in self-enhancement theory (Liu, Lee, Hui, Kwan, & Wu, 2013), which postulates that when i-deals are granted towards employees, they feel valued by their employer and experience personal growth and an improvement of the self. Therefore, i-deals may be important for people because it enhances their self-esteem. Finally, Vidyarthi, Chaudhry, Anand, and Liden (2014) have argued that the effects of i-deals can be conceptualized from an entitlement perspective, indicating that employees may feel entitled to receiving i-deals, and therefore do not necessarily reciprocate the successful negotiation of an i-deal with higher commitment or performance. Hence, perceptions of entitlement as a basis for i-deals preclude that employees will always respond to i-deals with favorable attitudes and behaviors towards the organization.

Despite the growing body of research on i-deals, there are a number of issues regarding the conceptualization and the applications of i-deals in the workplace, as well as the role of co-workers in the i-deal negotiation process. The aim of this book therefore is threefold; first, the book aims to provide further conceptual clarity regarding the concept of i-deals in the workplace. While Rousseau's (2001, 2005) seminal publications on i-deals have inspired research, the body of knowledge that has been generated by recent empirical research on i-deals can serve as a guide to further understanding of the concept, as well as to build new avenues for research on i-deals. It is notable that research on i-deals has emerged in conjunction with the rise of individualized perspectives on job design (Grant & Parker, 2009), including heightened interest in employee proactivity, job crafting, and protean careers. The central assumption of these concepts is the attention to the individual experience of the employee, who no longer follows a standardized career trajectory but for whom everything at work is an individualized experience that might or might not be shared by others. Hence, job adaptations currently follow an individualized approach, and research has been influenced profoundly by this trend. The question, however, is to which extent i-deals are any different, contributing to and enriching other existing constructs such as psychological contract, proactivity, and job crafting. Moreover, i-deals have not arisen in a social vacuum, but are the result and have been influenced by various societal processes. It is therefore necessary to disentangle the origins of i-deals, the functioning of i-deals in the workplace, and the conceptualization and research on i-deals. Therefore, the first part of the book will consider these issues to shed more light on the concept of i-deals.

The second aim of the book is to explore the applications of i-deals in the workplace. As stated, i-deals have not been developed in isolation, but exist within a broader framework of the employment relationship, and researchers have used multiple concepts to understand how employees experience their employment in relation to the i-deals they have negotiated with their employer. For instance, questions can be raised concerning the role of i-deals within employee career development as well as the role of strategic HRM for the enactment of i-deals in organizations. I-deals can be used as an important tool for both organizations and employees themselves to facilitate career development, yet there is only marginal evidence for this notion (Bal et al., 2012). Moreover, while i-deals are essentially part of the practices an organization applies, there is also very limited knowledge on how an organization can integrate principles of i-deals in larger human resource management systems (Rousseau, 2005). This book therefore aims to disentangle the role of i-deals within the broader employment relationship between the employee and the organization through focusing on areas of career development trajectories and the role of the organization and its HR systems.

The third and final aim of the book is to elucidate the role of co-workers in the negotiation and functioning of i-deals. Even though it has been mentioned that co-workers play an important role in i-deals (Rousseau, 2005), there has been only one study that investigated empirically how co-workers react to them (Lai et al., 2009). It is of crucial importance to advance understanding of the role of co-workers in the i-deal negotiation process in order to ascertain the conditions under which i-deals can be more and less successful. The third part of our book therefore aims to unravel how colleagues influence i-deal making and how colleagues react to i-deals. In sum, this book will advance understanding regarding the conceptualization and application of i-deals, and will in detail explore the role of co-workers in the i-deal making process.

Overview of the book

As stated, the book consists of three parts. The first part of the book is devoted to a conceptual investigation of the concept of i-deals, and the authors of these chapters explore how i-deals have been developed within a societal context, how i-deals have emerged within organizational contexts, and how i-deals have been developed in a scientific context by researchers. Subsequently, the second part of the book is devoted to applications of i-deals into the workplace. The central issue around this part of the book is to show how i-deals are used and can be used in organizations and by employees themselves. Hence, the chapters explore how i-deals can be integrated with career development and strategic HRM. The final part of the book explores the role of the immediate environment around the employee who negotiates an i-deal and discusses how i-deals function within groups and reactions of colleagues towards i-deals. Below, we will outline each of the chapters in our book.

In Chapter 2 by Matthijs Bal and Xander Lub, the authors discuss how i-deals have been the product of societal changes. They explain that i-deals have most notably been influenced by the individualization of society through which employees have focused more and more on their individual employment conditions with their organization. However, the prominence of neoliberalism as the current economic-political ideology in society also shapes the way organizations and employees negotiate i-deals, as well as the likelihood among employees to be able to negotiate i-deals. The chapter introduces a societal context of the rise and use of i-deals in organizations.

Chapter 3 by Sylvie Guerrero and Kathleen Bentein discusses how i-deals can be used by organizations to repair damaged relationships. In line with previous research by for instance Anand and colleagues (2010), Guerrero and Bentein explain that employment relationships nowadays have become more fragile and subject to psychological contract breaches, injustice, and discrimination. Organizations can use i-deals to repair those damaged relationships, and the authors explain in their chapter how organizations can do that and what the underlying theoretical processes are, as well as the conditions under which i-deals are expected to be effective in repairing damages from previous events in employment relationships.

The book continues with Chapter 4 by Neil Conway and Jacqueline Coyle-Shapiro, who critically review the concept of i-deals and i-deal research. The authors argue that definitions of i-deals, research on i-deals, and measurement of i-deals have so far been lacking precision and have several shortcomings. The authors review the research available on i-deals, and conclude that i-deals research could be strengthened in various ways, including in the research designs, but also in the way i-deals are conceptualized and investigated. One of the important questions the authors raise is whether i-deals actually benefit the two main parties involved: employees and organizations.

From the theoretical exploration of i-deals in relation to society and existing employment relationships at work, the book moves on to discuss the application of i-deals in the workplace. Chapter 5 by Aukje Nauta and Cristel van de Ven discusses the role of i-deals in career development. Through using an example of an employee in one organization, the authors explain how both employees and organizations can use i-deals to facilitate career development. They discuss why i-deals can be very important for the concept of career development and the ways organizations can manage i-deals in relation to career development. Especially by using an applied method of the dialogue in which employees with their managers openly communicate about mutual wishes for career development, i-deals can be negotiated that are fair to others and just in the sense of broader principles.

Chapter 6 by Brigitte Kroon, Charissa Freese, and René Schalk discusses the application of i-deals in the context of strategic human resource management. The authors explain how i-deals can be used within the broader context of the strategic goals an organization has, and more specifically they explain the positioning of i-deals within the practices of the organization. For instance, while organizations may offer on the organizational level employment conditions that apply to every employee, on the group or team level, resources may be offered that are specific to some groups only. I-deals refer to deals granted to individual employees, but they will always interact with higher-level employment conditions.

From the applications of i-deals within organizations, the book moves to Part III, which covers the role of the immediate context around the i-dealer. Employees negotiating i-deals communicate with their managers about the i-deal and also have co-workers involved in the process of i-deal negotiation. Smriti Anand and Prajya Vidyarthi discuss in Chapter 7 the role of i-deals within the group context and, more specifically, how leaders are essential in the distribution and management of i-deals in organizations. It is explained that i-deals are to a large extent dependent upon the relation between leaders and employees, but that it is likely that the *relative* quality of the relationship in comparison to other employees is particularly important for the likelihood of getting an i-deal by employees. Finally, it is not only the leader who matters, but also the context, such as the dominant culture within a team or organization.

Chapter 8 by Elise Marescaux and Sophie de Winne explores the role of justice in i-deal negotiation. The authors argue that i-deals can only be truly successful when all the parties involved benefit from the i-deal: employee, organization, and co-workers. In their empirical chapter, they investigate the role of justice and postulate that co-workers will perceive an i-deal to be more just when it's equitable and when the i-dealer needs the i-deal. However, in their study they show that these assumptions are contingent upon the type of i-deal (universalistic vs. particularistic) and gender. Hence, the authors show that for i-deals to be successful, it is imperative that co-workers perceive them as just.

The book finishes with Chapter 9 by Matthijs Bal and Denise Rousseau, which highlights the key issues regarding the conceptualization and applications of i-deals in the workplace. The chapter summarizes all of the main themes emerging from the book and discusses future research areas for i-deals. Based on the various chapters in this book and the summary in the end, researchers and practitioners gain more information as to how to study i-deals, investigate their antecedents and consequences, and take contextual factors into account. In sum, the book presents the state of the art in i-deals research and offers the reader an inspiring account of the future of i-deals in the workplace.

Note

1 Matthijs Bal, University of Bath, Bath, United Kingdom, p.m.bal@bath.ac.uk; Denise M. Rousseau, Carnegie Mellon University, Pittsburgh, USA, denise@cmu.edu.

References

Allen, T.D., Johnson, R.C., Kiburz, K.M., & Shockley, K.M. (2013). Work–family conflict and flexible work arrangements: Deconstructing flexibility. *Personnel Psychology, 66*(2), 345–376.

Anand, S., Vidyarthi, P.R., Liden, R.C., & Rousseau, D.M. (2010). Good citizens in poor-quality relationships: Idiosyncratic deals as a substitute for relationship quality. *Academy of Management Journal, 53*(5), 970–988.

Bal, P.M., De Jong, S.B., Jansen, P.G.W., & Bakker, A.B. (2012). Motivating employees to work beyond retirement: A multi-level study of the role of i-deals and unit climate. *Journal of Management Studies, 49*, 306–331.

Bal, P.M., & Jansen, P.G.W. (2014). Idiosyncratic deals for older workers: increased heterogeneity among older workers enhances the need for i-deals. In P.M. Bal, D.T.A.M. Kooij, & D.M. Rousseau (Eds.), *Aging workers and the employee–employer relationship*. Amsterdam: Springer.

Baltes, B.B., Briggs, T.E., Huff, J.W., Wright, J.A., & Neuman, G.A. (1999). Flexible and compressed workweek schedules: A meta-analysis of their effects on work-related criteria. *Journal of Applied Psychology, 84*(4), 496–513.

Blau, P.M. (1964). *Exchange and power in social life*. New York: Transaction.

Gouldner, A.W. (1960). The norm of reciprocity: A preliminary statement. *American Sociological Review*, 161–178.

Grant, A.M., & Parker, S.K. (2009). Redesigning work design theories: The rise of relational and proactive perspectives. *Academy of Management Annals, 3*(1), 317–375.

Greenberg, J., Roberge, M., Ho, V.T., & Rousseau, D.M. (2004). Fairness in idiosyncratic work arrangements: Justice as an i-deal. In J.J. Martocchio (Ed.), *Research in personnel and human resources management* (Vol. 23, pp. 1–34). Amsterdam: Elsevier.

Hornung, S., Rousseau, D.M., & Glaser, J. (2008). Creating flexible work arrangements through idiosyncratic deals. *Journal of Applied Psychology, 93*(3), 655–664.

Hornung, S., Rousseau, D.M., & Glaser, J. (2009). Why supervisors make idiosyncratic deals: Antecedents and outcomes of i-deals from a managerial perspective. *Journal of Managerial Psychology, 24*(8), 738–764.

Kooij, D.T.A.M., Rousseau, D.M., & Bal, P.M. (2014). Conclusions and future research. In P.M. Bal, D.T.A.M. Kooij, & D.M. Rousseau (Eds.), *Aging workers and the employee-employer relationship*. Amsterdam: Springer.

Lai, L., Rousseau, D.M., & Chang, K.T.T. (2009). Idiosyncratic deals: Coworkers as interested third parties. *Journal of Applied Psychology, 94*(2), 547–556.

Liu, J., Lee, C., Hui, C., Kwan, H.K., & Wu, L.-Z. (2013). Idiosyncratic deals and employee outcomes: The mediating roles of social exchange and self-enhancement and the moderating role of individualism. *Journal of Applied Psychology, 98*(5), 832–840.

Miner, A.S. (1987). Idiosyncratic jobs in formalized organizations. *Administrative Science Quarterly, 32*, 327–351.

Rosen, C.C., Slater, D.J., Chang, C.-H., & Johnson, R.E. (2013). Let's make a deal: Development and validation of the ex post i-deals scale. *Journal of Management, 39*(3), 709–742.

Rousseau, D.M. (1995). *Psychological contracts in organizations: Understanding written and unwritten agreements*. New York: Sage.

Rousseau, D.M. (2001). The idiosyncratic deal: Flexibility versus fairness? *Organizational Dynamics, 29*(4), 260–273.

Rousseau, D.M. (2005). *I-deals: Idiosyncratic deals employees bargain for themselves*. New York: ME Sharpe.

Rousseau, D.M., Ho, V.T., & Greenberg, J. (2006). I-deals: Idiosyncratic terms in employment relationships. *Academy of Management Review, 31*(4), 977–994.

Rousseau, D.M., Hornung, S., & Kim, T.G. (2009). Idiosyncratic deals: Testing propositions on timing, content, and the employment relationship. *Journal of Vocational Behavior, 74*(3), 338–348.

Vidyarthi, P.R., Chaudhry, A., Anand, S., & Liden, R.C. (2014). Flexibility i-deals: How much is ideal? *Journal of Managerial Psychology, 29*(3), 246–265.

2
INDIVIDUALIZATION OF WORK ARRANGEMENTS

A contextualized perspective on the rise and use of i-deals

Matthijs Bal and Xander D. Lub[1]

Introduction

Research on idiosyncratic deals (i-deals) has flourished during the last decade, since the seminal publications of Rousseau (2001, 2005). I-deals are increasingly popular among organizations and have been related to employee commitment (Hornung, Rousseau, & Glaser, 2008; Liu, Lee, Hui, Kwan, & Wu, 2013), job satisfaction (Rosen, Slater, Chang, & Johnson, 2013), and organizational citizenship behaviors (Anand, Vidyarthi, Liden, & Rousseau, 2010). Hence, the general tenet of i-deal research is that i-deals benefit employees and organizations (Rousseau, Ho, & Greenberg, 2006). This is also reflected in the definition of the concept; when an i-deal does not benefit the organization, it is no longer an i-deal, but preferential treatment by the organization towards an employee, examples being favoritism or cronyism or partiality towards friends in the organization. In the literature, our own work included (Bal, De Jong, Jansen, & Bakker, 2012; Van der Meij & Bal, 2013), there is a dominance of thinking of the beneficial effects of i-deals in the workplace for employees and organizations and a bias towards positive effects on work outcomes. Even though there has been some work on negative reactions, such as colleagues who might perceive unfairness regarding the distribution of i-deals (Greenberg, Roberge, Ho, & Rousseau, 2004; Lai, Rousseau, & Chang, 2009), we observe a tendency among researchers to be positive about the potential effects of i-deals for both employees and organizations. For instance, the recent study of Liu et al. (2013) concludes that i-deals result in *payoffs* for the organization in terms of commitment and proactive behaviors (italics added). This positive outlook may have resulted from a broader societal trend of individualism (Oyserman, Coon, & Kemmelmeier, 2002) and the resulting positioning of the individual at the center of the employment relationship. A risk of this approach, however, is a negligence of the broader context with respect to the dynamics of i-deals in the workplace. This is related to what has been referred to as the "psychologicalization" of employment relations (Godard, 2014), which is an increasing tendency to focus on employees as individuals negotiating employment with organizations, thereby ignoring the role of the collective (e.g., through representation, trade unions, or institutions). Moreover, recent societal changes include a greater emphasis on self-reliance of employees to take care of their careers and well-being (Olson, 2013). In response to this, the aim of this chapter is to explore the impact societal changes have had on i-deals and to discuss how contextual factors have impacted the rise and use of i-deals in the workplace. To do so, we discuss the trend of individualization of society, which has ultimately led to individualization of the workplace, providing the necessary ground for i-deals in the workplace.

Individualization and i-deals in the workplace

Rousseau (2001, 2005; Rousseau et al., 2006) coined the term i-deals to describe the voluntary, personalized agreements between individual employees and their organization. The term i-deal refer to an idiosyncratic deal, but it also refers to an i-deal being *ideal* in the sense that they should benefit both parties to the employment exchange: the employee and the organization. I-deals have been found to positively relate to various work outcomes, including commitment, satisfaction, organizational citizenship behaviors (OCBs), and the motivation to continue working beyond retirement (Anand et al., 2010; Bal et al., 2012; Hornung et al., 2008; Liu et al., 2013; Rosen et al., 2013; Van der Meij & Bal, 2013). However, at the same time, many studies have shown that the effects of i-deals are contingent, that is, effects may occur or not occur depending on contextual factors (Bal et al., 2012). For instance, Rosen and colleagues (2013), who developed a four-dimensional scale of the types of i-deals employees may negotiate with their employer, showed that depending on the type of i-deal, relationships with outcomes may be stronger or not present at all. Bal and colleagues (2012) showed that while flexibility i-deals related to higher motivation to continue working, the relations of development i-deals only manifested under conditions of favorable unit climate. In contrast, a study of Hornung and colleagues (2011) showed that while development i-deals related to higher work engagement, flexibility i-deals related to lower work–family conflict (see also Hornung et al., 2008). Hence, it is striking that across studies, researchers tend to find contrasting effects of i-deals, which may not only depend upon the type of i-deal employees negotiate with their organization, but also the context in which the i-deals are negotiated. Previous research on psychological contracts has shown that social referents play an important role in the constitution of psychological contracts employees have (Ho & Levesque, 2005). Hence, it is likely that i-deal negotiation draws upon the same processes and is equally influenced by social referents, and thus employees use information from the broader context in negotiating i-deals. While employees may be supported or hindered by their direct environment, such as coworkers, managers, and family, we will argue in this chapter that i-deals are both the *result* of societal trends and are *influenced by* societal trends, particularly in the current global economic crisis. To do so, we will first elaborate on the theoretical assumptions underlying the functioning of i-deals in the workplace.

Theory of i-deals

I-deals theorizing has been primarily based upon social exchange theory (Blau, 1964) and the norm of reciprocity (Gouldner, 1960). The basis of i-deals is established within the exchange relationship between employee and organization. I-deals serve as a key indicator for the relation between the two parties, and they are assumed to strengthen the employee–employer relationship over time. When the organization grants an i-deal to the employee, the employee will be likely to return the favorable treatment by the employer through becoming more committed, putting in more effort into the job, and an increased willingness to stay with the company. In line with the norm of reciprocity, employees are expected to return i-deals with higher motivation and performance. I-deals are important for employees, because they can facilitate a greater correspondence between their work and their selves (Bal et al., 2012; Baltes, Briggs, Huff, Wright, & Neuman, 1999). I-deals can facilitate employees to better balance work and nonwork, obtain more energy to perform, and reap more rewards from work. Hence, i-deals can fulfill the basic needs that people have, such as the needs for autonomy, competence and relatedness (Ryan & Deci, 2000). Through negotiation of individualized work arrangements, employees are no longer dependent upon the availability of practices within the system, but have the opportunity to negotiate resources that are important to the employee beyond existing regulations, for instance as prescribed by law, collective labor agreements or HR policies. Hence, i-deals may constitute a beneficial implementation of individualization in the workplace. This emphasis of the positive aspects of individualization at work has been manifested in various research areas, including proactivity (Grant & Parker, 2009), job crafting (Tims & Bakker, 2010), protean careers (Hall, 2004), and job redesign (Hornung, Rousseau, Glaser, Angerer, & Weigl, 2010). The tenet of these research streams is that people can distinguish themselves from other people through standing out, outperforming others, and anticipating changes at work through taking steps before others do. Research has shown that similar to the results obtained by research on i-deals, the effects of these types of behaviors are related to various positive work outcomes, including commitment, performance, and objective career success (Ng, Eby, Sorensen, & Feldman, 2005; Thomas, Whitman, & Viswesvaran, 2010). However, while researchers stress the fundamental benefits of proactivity and individual approaches at work, there is too little emphasis on the origin of this process, as well as the inherent (negative) side effects of such an approach to work and job design. Our main point here is therefore to argue that i-deals cannot be separated from their ideological origin or from the individualization of society combined with a dominant economic–political ideology of neoliberalism that currently exists within our societies.

Individualization of societies and its impact on work

Individualization of work arrangements is profoundly influenced by a number of societal trends, which can be traced back to the 1700s and the work of German philosopher Immanuel Kant. Kant proposed that human beings should be treated as ends in itself and not as means towards an end. According to his philosophy, the dignity of the human being is a categorical imperative, a principle that is intrinsically valid, or good in itself. Hence, an individual human being has a dignity that cannot be merely violated in order to achieve some end. His philosophy combined with an interest in the 1800s for the individual experience of the world, notable for instance in the poetry of Henry David Thoreau, has led to a conceptualization of society as consisting of individual human beings rather than collectives (Oyserman et al., 2002). The rise of psychology as a scientific discipline in the late 1800s also emphasized the increased attention for the individual. A central idea of this movement is that individuals are not just a part of a larger collective, such as a village or an ethnic group, but rather that individuals are persons with rights, such as the right to pursue one's self-interests. A collectivistic culture assumes the sacrifice of the individual for the collective, as can been seen in principle in various political ideologies, such as Marxism and social democracy in the times of Nazi Germany, and more recently in the sacrifice of suicide bombers in the Middle East for a greater purpose. The essence of collectivism is that the individual does not have an entitlement above the existence of the collective. However, Kantian philosophy assumes the dignity of the human being and respect for the fundamental right of each human being towards its dignity. An individualized human being has a psyche that experiences the world uniquely. In combination with the rise of psychoanalysis, psychology has grown dramatically after the 1900s.

But it was not only the rise of individualism in the 1900s that ultimately led to the particular interest in individualization at work. After the Second World War, and in particular in the late 1970s and early 1980s, the US and the UK, and to a certain extent Europe and other parts of the world as well, have been influenced profoundly by the upcoming capitalism under a neoliberal political ideology. In conjunction with the existing economic–political capitalist paradigm, a new order was established in the Western world which became increasingly dominated by the ideology of neoliberalism (Van Apeldoorn & Overbeek, 2012). Neoliberalism is an economic–political ideology whose central aim is to create economic freedom for people and organizations, thereby deregulating the economy, whilst it proposes trust in the free market to regulate itself. In this ideology, distribution of resources should not be regulated by government but should be governed by the invisible hand of the free market (Jessop, 2002). This invisible hand of the market is proposed to ensure the economic order. Interference of the government in the economic order is highly unwanted, unless it benefits existing large multinational corporations (Harvey, 2005). Neoliberalism aims to deregulate various types of services that traditionally are taken care of by the government, such as health care, education, infrastructure, and energy supply. Competition within these markets will, as the ideology prescribes, ensure that customers will benefit from the best quality for the lowest prices. The grounding principle of neoliberalism (and capitalism) is that individuals aspire to profit maximization; to do so, individuals make rational, strategic choices concerning how they obtain resources. As research has shown, this assumption is false and misleading (Sedlacek, 2011), but nonetheless neoliberalism has infiltrated the economic system throughout the world (Harvey, 2005). This has been particularly notable for instance in the European Union, which is founded based on neoliberal principles of the free market and deregulation of public services. Especially in the current economic crisis, Eurocratic officials stress the need to deregulate public services in suffering countries, such as Greece, Spain and Portugal, risking a similar process that has occurred with competition in the existing open markets. One of the major consequences of an economic system that stresses the human need for profit maximization and the pursuance of self-interest is the creation of a strong distinction between winners and losers (or haves and have-nots). Winners in this system are those people and organizations who achieve material and financial success and who are able to show the world a social status based upon the extrinsic success they have. Losers in this system are those people who have no economic success, because of some reason that limits them from achieving this. Reasons may include the inability to achieve success through lack of resources, education or skills, the lack of motivation or bad luck.

One of the consequences of a neoliberal society is hence the intensification of the distinction between winners and losers. As research has shown, the divide between the rich and the poor has increased substantially over the last decades (Global Post, 2013), a process also referred to as the Matthew Effect (Hornung et al., 2011; see also Chapter 5 by Nauta and van de Ven and Chapter 6 by Kroon et al., this volume). This effect describes the process in which people who are doing well receive better resources to improve than people in poorer situations, who lack those skills and opportunities. For instance, highly employable employees will be better able to negotiate i-deals, as they have many employment alternatives in contrast to employees with low employability. We observe a similar phenomenon on the societal level, with large and successful organizations in the current economy having more power to influence political decision making (Harvey, 2005), and hence to improve their own position through influencing decision-making processes that favor themselves over others, who consequently find themselves in impoverished circumstances. The winners, hence, are the people and large organizations that have benefited from the economic crisis as well. This process is also manifested in the social domain, where the emphasis on material success has dominated the decades after the Second World War until the economic crisis that started in 2008. People obtained social status primarily based on their economic success in society, and those people who were unsuccessful suffered. The consequence of the individualization of the public sphere has been an increasing emphasis on self-reliance and the responsibility of each individual for his or her own well-being. Individualization has thus decentralized responsibility for material and immaterial success to the individual. For instance, trade unions are having difficulties in sustaining their relevance in contemporary society, because they are representing a smaller portion of the workforce (i.e., primarily the Baby Boomers) and because younger workers do not realize the importance of collective representation (Bal, 2014; Godard, 2014). Hence, in an individualized society, every individual human being is responsible for his or her own welfare, but at the same time can no longer rely upon institutions to represent the needs and stakes of workers. Moreover, when governmental institutions are increasingly dominated by large organizations, workers have less control over their own workplace as well as their work conditions. For instance, a company like Apple can produce cheaply in China where poorer working conditions are the norm, and at the same time use tax havens (such as the Netherlands and Ireland) in order to pay as little tax as possible on their profits (Lucas, Kang, & Li, 2013; Tegenlicht, 2013). It also has been proven to be difficult to change the current system; pressure on the Dutch government to end the tax haven status has been counteracted by the organizations that profit from the current system (Tegenlicht, 2013). Hence, the profits that organizations make are increasingly unfairly distributed. In sum, individualization in combination with a dominant neoliberal ideology has created a society in which unfair distribution is the norm, and we argue that this is reflected in how i-deals currently function within the workplace.

Turning to the employment relationship between the employee and the organization, it can be argued that to be treated as a human being is a crucial element within the employment relationship (Barresi, 2010). In a neoliberalized world, however, where profitability becomes the most important raison d'être for an organization, many employees face the risk to be a mere link in the chain in the machinery of organizational functioning, ultimately leading to Marxist alienation from work, which nowadays is also called burnout. From this perspective, there is a neoliberal pressure on standardization and efficiency. Organizations in a neoliberal society are competing against each other through focusing on the highest quality for the lowest prices. To obtain lower consumer prices, labor and production processes are standardized and work is arranged as efficiently as possible (Peck, Theodore, & Brenner, 2012). Hence, neoliberalism causes a trend towards standardization of work and strong responsibility of the employee for high productivity, while at the same time, the organization has all rights to punish the employee for substandard performance. A notable example of how this in practice unfolds is the Amazon distribution center. While Amazon is able to outperform regular bookshops and record stores, the low prices they offer result from a highly efficient and employee-unfriendly and -undignified work system (BBC, 2013). This is the ultimate consequence of a neoliberal system where organizations can freely violate the dignity of the employee to outcompete other organizations. The dividing line between winners and losers in a neoliberal society is amplified in the haves and have-nots in the workplace. In absence of institutions that offer protection of employees (such as trade unions), employees become highly self-reliant and, hence, dependent upon their abilities, willingness and opportunities to negotiate work arrangements. In other words, as Rousseau (2012) rightfully mentions, employment relationships, or psychological contracts, can only emerge if there is the concept of free will, or the choice of an individual to engage in employment or not. With harsh economic realities and increasing unemployment, the concept of free will in employment comes under more and more pressure. The question hence is whether people still have a free will when they can only accept inhumane work conditions or have no employment at all. Hence, a situation where employees have no free will, i-deals lose their relevance, as they are likely to be negotiated only in a situation where employees have some level of bargaining power.

I-deals in the workplace

I-deals have been described as the opportunity for personalization or customization of work arrangements that provide people with jobs and careers that are accommodated to their abilities, needs, and wishes (Hornung et al., 2010; Rousseau, 2005). This positive view on how i-deals function in the workplace can be sustained through reinforcement of the individual dignity of the employee. It can be argued that because the employment relationship is individualized, employees are no longer treated as means to an end, that is, as resources that are employed by organizations in order to fulfill an organizational goal, such as survival or profit making. Hence, employees who negotiate i-deals no longer feel treated as a number, but rather as an individual human being, thereby enhancing their individual human dignity (Barresi, 2010). Human beings differ in their needs, capabilities, wishes, and personalities, and when this is recognized by organizations, employees feel that their fundamental human needs are fulfilled (Taskin & Devos, 2005). In this sense, i-deals can indeed promote Kantian dignity: through i-deals people are no longer a nameless resource employed by the organization, but can maintain their dignity as a human being. Respect from the employer for the employee as a person is enhanced through the possibility to negotiate employment arrangements that are personalized to the situation of the employee. In other words, i-deals shape the possibility to add an ideological dimension to the employment relationship, through which employee commitment may be enhanced, and meaning of work is created (Bal & Vink, 2011).

However, a darker perspective on i-deals emerges when the broader context is taken into account, and in particular the neoliberal domination in society. More specifically, in a society that distinguishes between a small group of winners versus an increasing group of losers (see Global Post, 2013), an equal dividing line is created among those few employees who are capable to negotiate i-deals and the large majority of workers who do not have the availability or ability to negotiate favorable arrangements with their employer. Individualization at work consequently becomes the privilege of the elite, and i-deals serve to enhance satisfaction and meaningfulness for those who already were thriving within the system. Empirical support for this notion can be found in the consistent positive relationship between quality of the relationship between leader and the employee (LMX) and i-deals (Hornung et al., 2010; Rosen et al., 2013). Employees who have better relationships with their managers negotiate more or better i-deals. While the direction of this relationship is yet to be ascertained, it is important to realize that negotiation of i-deals may be to a great extent dependent upon the willingness of the employer and manager to grant an i-deal. From a power perspective, the ability to negotiate i-deals is dependent on the scarcity of the resources that an employee can offer to the organization. Hence, the employees who have stronger relationships, and who are better performers, have more bargaining power (Rousseau, 2005) and will be able to negotiate more favorable work arrangements. Power is a crucial determinant of successful i-deal negotiation, because the employees without power will not have enough ability or motivation to successfully negotiate, partly because of the limited alternatives (Mazei et al., 2015).

In this way, i-deal negotiation and individualization accentuate and represent the differences created by the neoliberal system, and one could argue that individualization, or the breakdown of institutionalized representation, is an inherent part of the neoliberal project (Olson, 2013; Peck, Theodore, & Brenner, 2009). When people lack the opportunities to individualize their work arrangements, while others do have ample opportunities, the differences between these groups are accentuated over time. In sum, a paradox of individualization is created, because as we explained, on the one hand, individualization may facilitate and promote greater dignity of work and the person conducting the work, while on the other hand, individualization enhances the need for each individual to become self-reliant and capable to negotiate work arrangements. The central need for employees in the contemporary workplace is therefore to be proactive; only those who proactively negotiate, build their careers, and think ahead will survive (Parker, Bindl, & Strauss, 2010). Often ignored is the position of the less privileged and the nonproactive people in the workplace, since they become dependent upon others, and in a fully neoliberalized society, subject to the employer's whims.

I-deals in a societal context: looking ahead

Individualization is a societal change process that slowly unfolds over time and places (Inglehart, 1977, 1997). In combination with the dominance of a neoliberal ideology in society, a risk arises that i-deals serve the fortunate in society – those who are proactive and have the power to negotiate. I-deals have been framed as mutually beneficial for both employee and organization (Rosen et al., 2013; Rousseau et al., 2006). However, the basis for benefits is unclear, and even though studies have been conducted on the crucial role of coworker acceptance, there is still very little knowledge on how societal trends in general, and individualization and neoliberal thinking in particular, have an impact on i-deal negotiation. In fact, one of the major consequences of the global economic crisis that started in 2008 has been the enduring insecurity regarding economic–political models (Jessop, 2002; Peck et al., 2009, 2012). In other words, there is currently a change process unfolding, in which people will have to adapt to new economic realities. On the one hand, the dominant neoliberal paradigm is flourishing, as for instance is notable in the enormous pressure on austerity and deregulation in the European countries in order to respond to the challenges of the crisis. Hence, the neoliberal project is far from over and highly present, especially in the governmental domain, for example, in decision making and the interweaving of large organizations with governments (Ferguson, 2009). On the other hand, a societal change process is occurring with an increasing number of people who are openly questioning the sustainability of the current neoliberal, capitalist paradigm that operates in most of the countries throughout the world. However, the alternative to capitalism has traditionally been communism or Marxism, which is no real viable alternative according to most scholars (Sedlacek, 2011). Hence, there is a need to formulate sustainable alternatives to neoliberalism, in which people can experience cohesion beyond the individualism of pursuing self-interests only and a system that provides explicit attention to nonmonetary values, which are essentially ignored by neoliberalism. In relation to this, a future of i-deals and individualization at work is dependent upon the position of the individual in the organization. If neoliberalism prevails, there will be a growing dividing line between the rich and the poor, the winners and the losers and between employees who have access to i-deals and those who have not. However, if a viable alternative is emerging, another future for i-deals is foreseeable.

A strong resentment against the current economic–political system was present in the Occupy Wall Street movement that spread throughout the Western world in September 2011. The movement showed an increasing disapproval of the current system and the need for a new paradigm. The unequal distribution of wealth was a major concern, as well as the focus on profit maximization as the foundation of economic activity. An alternative system which revalues a more equal distribution of resources and other values besides profit making is slowly emerging. Economic models that presume individuals as pursuing only self-interest especially put pressure on our sense of cohesion and empathy for those who are not able to obtain economic success (Olson, 2013). Hence, alternatives are emerging in which specific attention is devoted to the role of cohesion among people with a great role for sustainability of new models (Bal, 2014; Bal & Jansen, 2015). First, a new model with a profile distinct from the current one is emerging, and it is based on the principle of human dignity (Killmister, 2010). In this new economic paradigm, each and every economic activity aims to maintain and promote human dignity. Human dignity is defined as the unalienable right of each human being to self-respect and respect from others, to set one's own standards and principles, and to live accordingly (Lucas et al., 2013; Sjoukes, 2012). The concept of human dignity has been developed by Kant and implies a free will of the human being. Human dignity is a fundamental human right, but at the same time, it is a fundamental human duty to behave dignified and not violate the dignity of other people. Hence, when an organization treats its employees in an indecent manner, the employees may feel that their dignity has been violated, while organizations may perceive this violation of human dignity as being permitted within the current neoliberal system. Central to the concept of human dignity is the principle of reciprocity: one not only has the right to be treated with dignity, but also the duty to treat others with dignity, and hence, human dignity forms the foundation of interpersonal relations.

This implies that the outcome of interpersonal relations can be profitable, but that the result of interpersonal contact should not be prioritized above the value of the contact, the relation, itself. Accordingly, the relation between two people, for instance through work where one accepts work for another party in return for payment, forms a value in itself, rather than a means towards profit. Definitions and scientific work on human dignity have so far been rather problematic and complex (Carozza, 2008; Misztal, 2012). For instance, human dignity has been operationalized in the Universal Declaration of Human Rights, Article 23 (Misztal, 2012). It has to be acknowledged, however, that this declaration has been the result of a compromise, and although it is the result of historical evolution of the value of the concept, it is still underdefined and underspecified. Moreover, individual human dignity exists within the experience of a person perceiving to be treated with or without dignity, and is therefore impossible to define in unambiguous terms. A consequence of this is that i-deals by definition cannot be ascertained as being dignified or taking dignity away from an individual person.

As a general rule, it can be stated that negotiated i-deals between an employee and an organization should not violate the dignity of the parties involved, being employees, employers, and coworkers (Greenberg et al., 2004). When some employees are able to negotiate and obtain valuable resources that are consequently withheld from other workers, it is not only a situation in which unfairness arises, but also one in which a violation of human dignity could occur (Lai et al., 2009). For instance, in a bank where the CEO is able to obtain huge bonuses while at the same time thousands of employees are laid off, there is no fundamental objection from a neoliberal ideology (instead it would fit a neoliberal ideology), while a system based on human dignity principles can accuse these acts. In such a system, i-deals can be used to promote human dignity instead of creating even stronger differences between winners and losers.

Application of i-deals in organizations

The question arising from the analysis on the societal context, in which i-deals have become popular and used in organizations, is how to sustain i-deals in organizations without theorizing i-deals as being merely a tool for organizations to distinguish between employees on the basis of their potential contribution to sustain current neoliberal practices. In other words, organizational systems should take into account the dignity of the employee in its functioning. Hence, when strategic decisions are made as to how an organization should function, it no longer suffices to focus only on profitability of the firm, and with it shareholder value, as this might lead to severe violations of human dignity. In a similar vein, organizations that use i-deals to retain, attract, and reward employees should be aware that i-deals can be used to promote as well as to violate the dignity of employees (Lucas et al., 2013). As a consequence, i-deals form a crucial tool by organizations to either sustain neoliberalism and hypercapitalism or to promote an alternative perspective on the role and importance of employees in organizations. More specifically, i-deals can be used to reward the lucky few, sustaining the Matthew Effect (Hornung et al., 2011). This means that i-deals provide the winners among the employees the opportunity to extend their career success, obtaining both extrinsic and intrinsic outcomes. Thereby they leave the losers behind, who increasingly are left with marginalized, poorly paid jobs (Godard, 2014). Otherwise, i-deals can be used to promote an individualized approach towards management and organizing, whereby individual human beings have the experience of being treated as such, through which meaning of work, fulfillment, and well-being is enhanced. This implies that organizations sometimes have to make choices against profitability and shareholder interests. Instead they make choices which are societally more relevant in the long term. This approach is important in the human resource management context, as the focus has been primarily on universalism, or the idea that organizations should adopt a standardized approach towards human resource management, and with it, the employee (Purcell, 1999). Through offering so-called high-commitment HRM, organizations expect each and every employee to become better performers, despite its risks of increasing fatigue and having adverse effects on employee well-being (Van de Voorde, Paauwe, & Van Veldhoven, 2012). Although only limited evidence exists for this pressure on standardization, many organizations have adopted this idea that employees could be treated all the same. An apparent potential consequence of this approach could not only be a drop in commitment and well-being (Bal, Kooij, & De Jong, 2013; Van de Voorde et al., 2012), but also a greater alienation from work, higher burnout, and the disappearance of the meaning of work for employees. Hence, i-deals should be used carefully by organizations, such that they promote identification with work and organization rather than to accentuate differentiation between the privileged and the marginalized.

Conclusion

In this chapter, we have elucidated how i-deals and interest in i-deals research have been inspired and to a great extent caused by societal changes and trends. Due to individualization of society and an increase of interest in the individual experience, there has been the necessary ground in organizations to differentiate between individual employees, while the dominance of neoliberalism in contemporary society has stressed the difference between the privileged and the losers (Harvey, 2005). Both trends have profoundly shaped the forms and experiences of i-deals in organizations, and it could be argued that even the definition of i-deals has been influenced by these trends. It was already acknowledged in the preface of the seminal book on i-deals (Rousseau, 2005) that the decline of collective bargaining and the reduction of standard benefits have caused the need for workers to seek out the conditions of their employment themselves. However, there has been too little appreciation for how these changes have been accelerated by neoliberalism (Jessop, 2002). Hence, research on i-deals in organizations has implicitly followed this neoliberal paradigm, focusing on the benefits of i-deals for organizations (Hornung et al., 2009), as well as the pseudo-benefits for employees, which should ultimately primarily benefit the organization, such as employee commitment (Hornung et al., 2008), proactive behaviors (Liu et al., 2013), and job satisfaction (Rosen et al., 2013). In other words, investment in the employee through i-deals will pay off for organizations, because it enhances employee commitment, which in its turn relates to higher performance and lower turnover, and with it, decreased costs of turnover (Harrison, Newman, & Roth, 2006). For future research and application of i-deals in organizations, we suggest a number of directions.

First, i-deal definition and conceptualization should incorporate the stakes of various parties in the concept; every act of individualization within organizations cannot be conceptualized without taking the dominant neoliberal paradigm into account. It is therefore necessary to disentangle the concept of i-deals from its ideological confound, as individualization cannot only be used in order to sustain differences between winners and losers in society, but also to create meaning of work, fulfillment, and build cohesion among groups in society. Therefore, a more explicit conceptualization of i-deals (and with it individualization) as an act of meaning making, reconciliation and recognition of the individual within the collective can be a significant aid to a further understanding of the concept and its functioning in the workplace. Hence, the potential outcomes of i-deals should be expanded beyond the simplistic level of well-known employee attitudes and behaviors, such as satisfaction, commitment, and performance.

Second, a debate is warranted on the role of social justice in i-deals. While there is some research available on the role of individual justice within i-deals (Greenberg et al., 2004; Lai et al., 2009), there is no clarity as to the entitlement of i-deals in organizations. While i-deals have been defined and conceptualized as special deals negotiated by highly valued employees within organizations (see Rousseau, 2005; but also Chapter 4 by Conway and Coyle-Shapiro, this volume), recent research has also pointed towards more equal distribution of i-deals within organizations (Bal et al., 2012; but also Chapter 5 by Nauta and van de Ven, this volume). Hence, the question is whether entitlement to i-deals results from special contributions made to an organization, or the right to be treated as an individual human being. If the latter is granted more attention in research, new and important questions will arise, as for instance regarding the distribution of i-deals. If the right to be treated as an individual human being is conceptualized as the foundation of i-deals, a new stream of research could arise from this renewed conceptualization. Moreover, justice of i-deals will not be (only) framed in terms of coworker acceptance (i.e., perceived fairness of a negotiated i-deal), but also, and perhaps primarily, in terms of the achieved social justice, or the extent to which i-deals enhance an individualized, dignified experience of work, including the rights and integrity of others.

In sum, this chapter has discussed the societal context in which i-deals have arisen and are negotiated. It is important for research and practitioners alike that they understand the context of i-deals, and that i-deals can be used either to accentuate differences between employees or to resolve issues of social justice, and therefore can be used to create a dignified experience of work, in which the rights and duties of various parties in and around an organization are taken into account.

Note

1 Matthijs Bal, University of Bath, Bath, United Kingdom; Xander D. Lub, Saxion University of Applied Sciences, Deventer, the Netherlands, VU University, Amsterdam, the Netherlands.

References

Anand, S., Vidyarthi, P.R., Liden, R.C., & Rousseau, D.M. (2010). Good citizens in poor-quality relationships: Idiosyncratic deals as a substitute for relationship quality. *Academy of Management Journal, 53*(5), 970–988.

Bal, P.M. (2014). *Voorbij neoliberalisme in de arbeids- en organisatiepsychologie: Menselijke waardigheid en organisatiedemocratie* [Beyond neoliberalism in work and organizational psychology: Human dignity and workplace democracy]. Manuscript under review.

Bal, P.M., De Jong, S.B., Jansen, P.G.W., & Bakker, A.B. (2012). Motivating employees to work beyond retirement: A multi-level study of the role of i-deals and unit climate. *Journal of Management Studies, 49*, 306–331.

Bal, P.M., & Jansen, P.G.W. (2015). Idiosyncratic deals for older workers: Increased heterogeneity among older workers enhances the need for I-deals. In P.M. Bal, D.T.A.M. Kooij, & D.M. Rousseau (Eds.), *Aging workers and the employee–employer relationship* (pp. 129–144). Amsterdam: Springer.

Bal, P.M., Kooij, D.T., & De Jong, S.B. (2013). How do developmental and accommodative HRM enhance employee engagement and commitment? The role of psychological contract and SOC strategies. *Journal of Management Studies, 50*(4), 545–572.

Bal, P.M., & Vink, R. (2011). Ideological currency in psychological contracts: The role of team relationships in a reciprocity perspective. *International Journal of Human Resource Management, 22*(13), 2794–2817.

Baltes, B.B., Briggs, T.E., Huff, J.W., Wright, J.A., & Neuman, G.A. (1999). Flexible and compressed workweek schedules: A meta-analysis of their effects on work-related criteria. *Journal of Applied Psychology, 84*(4), 496–513.

Barresi, J. (2010). On seeing our selves and others as persons. *New Ideas in Psychology, 30*, 120–130.

BBC. (2013). Website accessed May 12, 2014. http://www.bbc.co.uk/programmes/b03k5kzp

Blau, P.M. (1964). *Exchange and power in social life*. New York: Transaction.

Carozza, P.G. (2008). Human dignity and judicial interpretation of human rights: A reply. *European Journal of International Law, 19*(5), 931–944.

Ferguson, J. (2009). The uses of neoliberalism. *Antipode, 41*(s1), 166–184.

Global Post. (2013). Website accessed May 12, 2014. http://www.globalpost.com/dispatch/news/regions/americas/united-states/130910/gap-between-us-rich-and-poor-reaches-record-widt

Godard, J. (2014). The psychologicalisation of employment relations? *Human Resource Management Journal, 24*, 1–18.

Gouldner, A.W. (1960). The norm of reciprocity: A preliminary statement. *American Sociological Review*, 161–178.

Grant, A.M., & Parker, S.K. (2009). Redesigning work design theories: The rise of relational and proactive perspectives. *Academy of Management Annals, 3*(1), 317–375.

Greenberg, J., Roberge, M., Ho, V.T., & Rousseau, D.M. (2004). Fairness in idiosyncratic work arrangements: Justice as an i-deal. In J.J. Martocchio (Ed.), *Research in personnel and human resources management* (Vol. 23, pp. 1–34). Amsterdam: Elsevier.

Hall, D.T. (2004). The protean career: A quarter-century journey. *Journal of Vocational Behavior, 65*(1), 1–13.

Harrison, D.A., Newman, D.A., & Roth, P.L. (2006). How important are job attitudes? Meta-analytic comparisons of integrative behavioral outcomes and time sequences. *Academy of Management Journal, 49*(2), 305–325.

Harvey, D. (2005). *A brief history of neoliberalism*. Oxford: Oxford University Press.

Ho, V.T., & Levesque, L.L. (2005). With a little help from my friends (and substitutes): Social referents and influence in psychological contract fulfillment. *Organization Science, 16*(3), 275–289.

Hornung, S., Glaser, J., Rousseau, D.M., Angerer, P., & Weigl, M. (2011). Employee-oriented leadership and quality of working life: Mediating roles of idiosyncratic deals. *Psychological Reports, 108*(1), 59–74.

Hornung, S., Rousseau, D.M., & Glaser, J. (2008). Creating flexible work arrangements through idiosyncratic deals. *Journal of Applied Psychology, 93*(3), 655–664.

Hornung, S., Rousseau, D.M., & Glaser, J. (2009). Why supervisors make idiosyncratic deals: Antecedents and outcomes of i-deals from a managerial perspective. *Journal of Managerial Psychology, 24*(8), 738–764.

Hornung, S., Rousseau, D.M., Glaser, J., Angerer, P., & Weigl, M. (2010). Beyond top-down and bottom-up work redesign: Customizing job content through idiosyncratic deals. *Journal of Organizational Behavior, 31*(2–3), 187–215.

Inglehart, R.F. (1977). *The silent revolution: Changing values and political styles among Western publics*. Princeton, NJ: Princeton University Press.

Inglehart, R. (1997). *Modernization and Postmodernization: Cultural, economic, and political change in 43 societies* (Vol. 19). Princeton, NJ: Princeton University Press.

Jessop, B. (2002). Liberalism, neoliberalism, and urban governance: A state-theoretical perspective. *Antipode, 34*, 452–472.

Killmister, S. (2010). Dignity: Not such a useless concept. *Journal of Medical Ethics, 36*, 160–164.

Lai, L., Rousseau, D.M., & Chang, K.T.T. (2009). Idiosyncratic deals: Coworkers as interested third parties. *Journal of Applied Psychology, 94*(2), 547–556.

Liu, J., Lee, C., Hui, C., Kwan, H.K., & Wu, L.-Z. (2013). Idiosyncratic deals and employee outcomes: The mediating roles of social exchange and self-enhancement and the moderating role of individualism. *Journal of Applied Psychology, 98*(5), 832–840.

Lucas, K., Kang, D., & Li, Z. (2013). Workplace dignity in a total institution: Examining the experiences of Foxconn's migrant workforce. *Journal of Business Ethics, 114*(1), 91–106.

Mazei, J., Hüffmeier, J., Freund, P. A., Stuhlmacher, A. F., Bilke, L., & Hertel, G. (2015). A meta-analysis on gender differences in negotiation outcomes and their moderators. *Psychological Bulletin, 141*, 85–104.

Misztal, B.A. (2012). The idea of dignity: Its modern significance. *European Journal of Social Theory, 16*(1), 101–121.

Ng, T.W., Eby, L.T., Sorensen, K.L., & Feldman, D.C. (2005). Predictors of objective and subjective career success: A meta-analysis. *Personnel Psychology, 58*(2), 367–408.

Olson, G. (2013). *Empathy imperiled: Capitalism, culture, and the brain*. New York: Springer.

Oyserman, D., Coon, H.M., & Kemmelmeier, M. (2002). Rethinking individualism and collectivism: Evaluation of theoretical assumptions and meta-analyses. *Psychological Bulletin, 128*(1), 3–72.

Parker, S.K., Bindl, U.K., & Strauss, K. (2010). Making things happen: A model of proactive motivation. *Journal of Management, 36*(4), 827–856.

Peck, J., Theodore, N., & Brenner, N. (2009). Postneoliberalism and its malcontents. *Antipode, 41*(s1), 94–116.

Peck, J., Theodore, N., & Brenner, N. (2012). Neoliberalism resurgent? Market rule after the great recession. *South Atlantic Quarterly, 111*, 265–288.

Purcell, J. (1999). Best practice and best fit: Chimera or cul-de-sac? *Human Resource Management Journal, 9*(3), 26–41.

Rosen, C.C., Slater, D.J., Chang, C.-H., & Johnson, R.E. (2013). Let's make a deal: Development and validation of the ex post i-deals scale. *Journal of Management, 39*(3), 709–742.

Rousseau, D.M. (2001). The idiosyncratic deal: Flexibility versus fairness? *Organizational Dynamics, 29*(4), 260–273.

Rousseau, D.M. (2005). *I-deals: Idiosyncratic deals employees bargain for themselves*. New York: M. E. Sharpe.

Rousseau, D.M. (2012). Free will in social and psychological contracts. *Society and Business Review, 7*, 8–13.

Rousseau, D.M., Ho, V.T., & Greenberg, J. (2006). I-deals: Idiosyncratic terms in employment relationships. *Academy of Management Review, 31*, 977–994.

Ryan, R.M., & Deci, E.L. (2000). Self-determination theory and the facilitation of intrinsic motivation, social development, and well-being. *American Psychologist, 55*(1), 68–78.

Sedlacek, T. (2011). *Economics of good and evil: The quest for economic meaning from Gilgamesh to Wall Street*. Oxford: Oxford University Press.

Sjoukes, S. (2012). *On working with dignity. Introducing the construct of human dignity to the field of organizational psychology by means of the clarity trial* (Unpublished dissertation, Erasmus University, Rotterdam).

Taskin, L., & Devos, V. (2005). Paradoxes from the individualization of human resource management: The case of telework. *Journal of Business Ethics, 62*(1), 13–24.

Tegenlicht. (2013). Website accessed May 12, 2014. http://tegenlicht.vpro.nl/afleveringen/2012-2013/tax-free-tour.html

Thomas, J.P., Whitman, D.S., & Viswesvaran, C. (2010). Employee proactivity in organizations: A comparative meta-analysis of emergent proactive constructs. *Journal of Occupational and Organizational Psychology, 83*(2), 275–300.

Tims, M., & Bakker, A.B. (2010). Job crafting: Towards a new model of individual job redesign. *South African Journal of Industrial Psychology, 36*(2), 1–9.

Van Apeldoorn, B., & Overbeek, H. (2012). The life course of the neoliberal project and the global crisis. In H. Overbeek & B. van Apeldoorn (Eds.), *Neoliberalism in crisis* (pp. 1–20). Hampshire: Palgrave Macmillan.

Van De Voorde, K., Paauwe, J., & Van Veldhoven, M. (2012). Employee well-being and the HRM–organizational performance relationship: A review of quantitative studies. *International Journal of Management Reviews, 14*(4), 391–407.

Van der Meij, K., & Bal, P.M. (2013). De ideale "idiosyncratic-deal": I-deals, "organizational citizenship behavior" en de invloed van de uitwisselings relatie tussen werknemers en werkgevers [The ideal "idiosyncratic deal": I-deals, organizational citizenship behavior, and the influence of exchange relationship between employees and employers]. *Gedrag & Organisatie, 26*(2), 156–181.

3
I-DEALS IN DAMAGED RELATIONSHIPS

Sylvie Guerrero and Kathleen Bentein[1]

I-deals in damaged relationships

Until now, research on i-deals has focused on the role of i-deals in positive employment relationships between the individual and the employer. Based on the assumption that i-deals provide access to valuable resources and send a signal that the employer values the employee and grants that person special treatment that other colleagues do not receive (e.g., Hornung, Rousseau, & Glaser, 2008; Rousseau, Hornung, & Kim, 2009), empirical studies have demonstrated that i-deals are positively associated with job satisfaction (Hornung, Glaser, & Rousseau, 2010a), organizational commitment (Hornung et al., 2008; Ng & Feldman, 2010), relational psychological contracts (Lee & Hui, 2011), and quality of the social exchange (Rousseau, Hornung, & Kim, 2009).

Less attention has been paid to the role of i-deals in a context where employment relationships are less positive. Dirks, Lewicki, and Zaheer (2009) used the term "damaged relationships" to refer to situations in which employees feel that their relationship with their employer is impacted by a transgression. Examples of damaged relationships include psychological contract breach and violation (Robinson, 1996; Morrison & Robinson, 1997), perceptions of injustice and discrimination (Goldman, Gutek, Stein, & Lewis, 2006), poor-quality relationships with the organization and the direct supervisor (Cropanzano & Mitchell, 2005), and conflicting relationships (Labianca, Brass, & Gray, 1998). Some preliminary empirical research on i-deals suggests that i-deals might compensate for the negative effects of damaged relationships. For example, Hornung, Rousseau, and Glaser (2009) suggested that supervisors might authorize i-deals as a means of remedying unfulfilled employer psychological contracts. They found a positive relationship between unfulfilled employer obligations and supervisor authorization of workload-reduction i-deals. Guerrero, Bentein, and Lapalme (2014) established that developmental i-deals counterbalance the loss of trust associated with psychological contract breaches and help maintain organizational commitment among a sample of high performers. Anand, Vidyarthi, Liden, and Rousseau (2010) found that developmental i-deals are more strongly related to organizational citizenship behaviors (OCBs) in a context of low leader-member exchange (LMX) and low team-member exchange (TMX), suggesting that i-deals can provide highly valued resources that compensate for poor-quality relationships with supervisors and colleagues.

Extending this line of research, this chapter further explores the processes through which i-deals can help repair employment relationships damaged by the employer, and discusses how the content, initiator, timing, and history of i-deals may moderate these processes.

I-deals and processes of relationship repair

I-deals are "special terms of employment *negotiated* between individual workers and their employers" (Rousseau, Ho, & Greenberg, 2006, p. 977). They are obtained through a bargaining process between the individual and the organization that leads to an explicit deal about specific elements of the employment relationship. This perspective highlights that i-deals can be used to modify and craft the employment relationship, through a formalized agreement, leading to observable and tangible changes in the employment relationship that should better suit individual and organizational needs (Hornung, Rousseau, Glaser, Angerer, & Weigl, 2010b; Rousseau et al., 2006).

We believe i-deals might offer opportunities to repair damaged relationships. Literature on relationship repair (e.g., Bottom, Gibson, Daniels, & Murnighan, 2002; Dirks et al., 2009; Tomlinson & Mayer, 2009) suggests that a variety of verbal responses (e.g., apologies, excuses, accounts, statements of remorse) and substantive actions (e.g., hostage posting, monitoring, new contracts) might be effective tactics for rebuilding damaged relationships. These tactics reflect repentance from the "violator" and forgiveness for the "victim" that are important to restart cooperation and maintain a bond between the two parties (Tomlinson, Dineen, & Lewicki, 2004). Dirks, Lewicki, and Zaheer (2009) argue that verbal and substantive tactics are effective because they trigger three processes or mechanisms through which relationships can be repaired: attributional, social equilibrium, and structural processes. We propose to adapt these three processes to the study of i-deals in damaged relationships.[2] The attributional process (Heider, 1958) focuses on the interpretation of the employer's intentions. In line with this process, we propose that i-deals can repair damage if the employee perceives that the employer experiences redemption following the transgression and did not damage the relationship intentionally (Tomlinson & Mayer, 2009). The social equilibrium process (Goffman, 1967) highlights that poor employment relationships threaten the relative standing of the employee in the organization (e.g., feelings of being viewed poorly by the organization) and the norms that govern the relationship (e.g., the norm of justice or mutual respect). Based on this argument, we propose that i-deals may repair damaged relationships by restoring the balance in the exchange between the two parties. The structural process addresses the contextual factors surrounding the relationship that enable individuals to exert greater control over the relationship and secure the employer's cooperation with future behaviors or decisions (Kim, Dirks, & Cooper, 2009; Molm, Takahashi, & Peterson, 2000). We focused on the perceived controllability suggested by Dirks et al. (2009) in this third process to study how i-deals may repair damaged relationships. We develop our arguments below.

First, negotiating i-deals involves verbal exchanges between the employer and the employee that may provide opportunities for verbal responses to the damage. The existence of a negotiation process indicates that the two parties voluntarily agree to change the employment relationship by introducing new promises and new forms of regulation (Hornung et al., 2008), which can be interpreted by protagonists as signals of repentance from the employer and of forgiveness from the employee. In addition, by authorizing i-deals, the employer sends the message that the organization is willing to change the relationship and that past damage may not happen in the future. By meeting individuals' salient needs with i-deal authorization (Rousseau et al., 2006), employers may also modify attributions regarding their intention to harm the employee and demonstrate that damage was not done intentionally or was beyond the organization's control (Guerrero et al., 2014). Therefore, negotiating i-deals may alter the cognitive sense-making attributed to the employment relationship by changing causal attribution (Weiner, 1986) of past damage.

Second, i-deals may restore the exchange balance by raising the relative standing of the employee and by reaffirming the idea that justice and equity norms govern the employee–organization relationship (Guerrero et al., 2014). I-deals are usually authorized by the organization as a sign of recognition of the employee's contributions (Rousseau et al., 2006) and of individual appreciation (Rousseau et al., 2009). By definition, and in contrast with standard deals, i-deals signal an interest in the individual's particular needs (Ng & Feldman, 2010). Employees who successfully negotiate an i-deal know that they are receiving special treatment and that other employees do not enjoy the same arrangements (Rousseau et al., 2006). These arrangements might increase their self-value in the organization (Ng & Feldman, 2010). This self-enhancement mechanism has been validated by Liu, Lee, Hui, Kwan, and Wu (2013), who found that flexibility and developmental i-deals maintain high levels of organizational commitment via perceptions of high organization-based self-esteem. I-deals may also influence the norms of justice and equity that are expected to govern the employment relationship (Guerrero et al., 2014). Employees may interpret the organization's authorizing an i-deal as an effort to increase the rewards provided to them and as willingness to ensure greater fairness in the allocation of organizational rewards for the employee's contribution (Guerrero et al., 2014). Hornung et al. (2010a) have shown that authorizing i-deals increases employees' perceptions of distributive justice. I-deals thus represent an opportunity to repair the exchange imbalance created by a damaged relationship by altering justice perceptions.

Third, i-deals can be seen as an example of an exchange of resources that, like policies or other substantive actions (Dirks et al., 2009; Kim et al., 2009), increases controllability in future exchanges. With i-deals, individuals increase their perceptions that the exchange relationship is secured through the negotiation of specific arrangements that satisfy organizational and individual needs (Mayer, Davis, & Schoorman, 1995; Molm et al., 2000). This idea is supported by Hornung et al. (2010b), who show that negotiation of task i-deals makes employees feel more in control of their jobs. Considering that perceived controllability influences the individual's response to a negative outcome (Weiner, 1986), the increased feeling of control enabled through i-deals should allow employees to maintain their relationship with the employer.

Through attributional, exchange balance, and perceived controllability processes, i-deals represent arrangements that might help repair damaged employment relationships. However, the power of i-deals to repair a damaged relationship may vary, depending, for instance, on the nature of the damage created in the relationship. For the purpose of this chapter, the next section focuses on the characteristics of i-deals negotiation that moderate the relationship between i-deals and the reparation degree of the employment relationship.

Conditions of the repairing power of i-deals

The content of i-deals

I-deals may be negotiated relative to a variety of resources available in the employment relationship, including pay, task, skills development, flexibility, work hours, work load, and personal support. Following Foa and Foa's (1975) classification of resource categories, the literature on i-deals (e.g., Anand et al., 2010; Guerrero et al., 2014; Hornung et al., 2008, 2009; Rousseau et al., 2006, 2009) distinguishes between i-deals related to concrete (tangible) and universal resources (having common meaning and values across contexts – e.g., money, work hours), and i-deals related to abstract (conveyed through verbal and paralinguistic behaviors) and particularistic resources (their meaning depends on their source and context – e.g., status, support, skills development). Based on this distinction, the content of i-deals can be ranked on a continuum from universal quantifiable resources to particularistic intangible resources.

The effects of negotiation of i-deals may differ depending on the content of the deals. Rousseau, Ho, and Greenberg (2006) argue that concrete and universal resources are the type of resources exchanged in economic and more transactional exchanges. Due to their concrete nature, they can be negotiated in exchange relationships where there is little trust and in poor employment relationships because they reflect the economic conditions of employment. Conversely, abstract and particularistic resources (e.g., a manager's support for a decision, career opportunities) satisfy socioemotional needs that are typical of long-term social exchanges (Rousseau et al., 2006; Rousseau et al., 2009). I-deals associated with abstract and particularistic resources are thus more relational in nature. Empirical research supports this assumption and establishes that i-deals concerning skills development are related to organizational affective commitment (Hornung et al., 2008; Liu et al., 2013) and to perceptions that the employment relationship favors social exchanges (Rousseau et al., 2009), while i-deals about work hours are linked to perceptions that the employment relationship is based on an economic exchange (Rousseau et al., 2009).

Past research on i-deal content implies that negotiating i-deals when a relationship has been damaged may have different reparatory effects depending on the content of the i-deals. The negotiation of concrete and universal resources may be used as a patch that maintains a connection through a partial restoration of the exchange balance, but does not send the employee a signal of the employer's redemption. In contrast, the negotiation of abstract and particularistic resources may be more useful for fixing a damaged relationship with the organization. By introducing elements of the job based on socioemotional needs to change the conditions of the employment relationship, intangible i-deals provide valuable resources that may alter the employee's perceptions of attribution. I-deals associated with intangible resources may also send a signal that the individual has high standing and high value to the employer (Anand et al., 2010) despite the perceived damage, which provides an opportunity for increasing the exchange balance. This idea is supported by empirical studies. Anand et al. (2010) concluded that developmental i-deals compensate for poor LMX and TMX to predict OCBs, while Guerrero et al. (2014) found that developmental i-deals help maintain organizational commitment despite perceptions of psychological contract breaches. These two empirical studies confirm the assumption that skills-development i-deals are likely to compensate for poor relationships.

Nonetheless, if the damage to the relationship is severe, it seems more unlikely that the employee will initiate bargaining for abstract and particularistic resources. The negotiation of such resources implies, by definition, a basic level of confidence in the partner's reliability and integrity or a basic level of trust, because it is difficult to clearly specify all aspects of these arrangements in advance. Relatedly, Hornung et al. (2009) found that to compensate for unfulfilled obligations, supervisors authorize i-deals related to workload reduction but not i-deals related to skills development or work flexibility. This result tends to indicate that supervisors may use more concrete i-deals to compensate for highly damaged relationships. These concrete and universal elements help to restore positive exchanges in the relationship (perceived controllability process), but might not be sufficient to repair trust in the long term.

Who initiates i-deals?

I-deals can be initiated by the employee or the employer (Rousseau et al., 2006). When i-deals are initiated by the employee, they represent a way to bargain value and appreciation from the employer (Rousseau, 2005). In the context of a damaged relationship, the individual may proactively ask for changes in the employment relationship (Hornung et al., 2008, 2009). Empirical research shows that in the context of a damaged relationship marked by psychological contract violation or poor job satisfaction, employees might use voice as a constructive effort or tactic to restore the relationship (Farrell, 1983; Turnley & Feldman, 1999). Using voice involves appealing to those in authority to correct the perceived injustice and restore positive exchanges (Hirschman, 1970). Initiating i-deal negotiation could be seen as a voice tactic that the employee uses following an employer transgression (Hornung et al., 2009). The individual wants the relationship to continue and looks for ways and signals that things can change. Successful negotiation indicates that the employer has listened to the employee's complaints, which may build a favorable context for repairing damage.

The employer can also initiate the i-deal bargaining process after a transgression of the relationship. The literature on trust repair shows that when attempting to repair a relationship, much depends on the employer response (Dirks et al., 2009; Tomlinson & Mayer, 2009). Offers of penance and apologies, coupled with interactions that go beyond the discussion of tasks (Clark & Sefton, 2001) are effective in restoring cooperation in a broken relationship (Gibson, Bottom, & Murnighan, 1999). Schweitzer, Hershey, and Bradlow (2006) also found that promising to change behaviors may modify the other party's perspective. The employers' proactive actions to repair the damaged relationship are thus important because they might signal that the employer acknowledges its mistakes, demonstrates redemption, and wants to change behaviors in the future (Bottom et al., 2002).

However, Ng and Feldman (2012) recently demonstrated that employer promises of future i-deals do not succeed in repairing the bonds between employee and employer, but may even exacerbate the negative reactions to breaches of past promises. They showed that promises of future i-deals from the employer moderated the negative effect of breaches of past promises on employees' affective organizational commitment, such that the negative effect is greatest when employees with poor job alternatives are promised future i-deals by the employer. They suggest that a potential explanation for their result is that employees tend to view past breaches as signals that the organization is not trustworthy and therefore that promises of future i-deals cannot be relied upon either. In this case, i-deals initiated by the employer might not always be effective in repairing relationships.

One approach to addressing this apparent contradiction comes from the trust repair literature, which suggests that the effectiveness of a future-oriented response will depend on how the transgression has been framed: as a matter of competence (i.e., skills and abilities required for a job) vs. as a matter of integrity (i.e., values or principles) (Kim et al., 2009; Kim, Dirks, Cooper, & Ferrin, 2006; Kim, Ferrin, Cooper, & Dirks, 2004). The trust repair literature has shown that voluntary substantive actions tend to repair trust more effectively when the transgression is attributed to lack of competence rather than poor values or lack of integrity (Ferrin, Kim, Cooper, & Dirks, 2007; Kim et al., 2004, 2006). We might therefore expect that promises of future i-deals initiated by the employee will be more successful after a transgression interpreted based on the employer's competence than when a transgression is seen as calling into question the employer's integrity or values. We propose that by initiating i-deal negotiation, the employer can demonstrate that it is able and willing to restore the relationship and that the damage can be reduced in the future. However, the repairing power of these future i-deals is likely to be effective only if the employee does not fully attribute the relationship damage to the employer's lack of integrity or poor values.

The timing of i-deals

After damage to a relationship, the timing of repairs matters: delayed efforts to repair the damage should have a lesser effect on the willingness to reconcile relationships than immediate responses (Tomlinson et al., 2004). While some negotiated i-deals may lead to immediate changes in the relationship and can be immediately fulfilled by the organization (e.g., receive a bonus, participate in a training program), other i-deals may not be fulfilled immediately (e.g., waiting for a promotion or a new mission). In the latter situation, i-deal fulfillment is delayed: the employee receives a promise (Ng & Feldman, 2012) that the relationship will change, which may be associated with a quantifiable or particularistic element of the relationship, but the employee is not certain that the promise will be fulfilled in the future.

The repairing power of i-deals may be different for existing i-deals and promises of future i-deals. Empirical research about fulfilled existing i-deals finds that these i-deals compensate for a poor relationship in maintaining organizational commitment (Guerrero et al., 2014) and high levels of OCBs (Anand et al., 2010). Thus the fact that negotiated i-deals can be fulfilled after the employee perceives damage in the employment relationship provides tangible evidence of damage repair that is likely to effectively counterbalance the negative effects of damage.

However, when i-deals are based on long-term promises, the employee does not have the same evidence of change. Verbal responses to damage can even be viewed as "cheap talk" when they are not accompanied by more tangible evidence of repentance from the employer (Farrell & Gibbons, 1989) or if the damage includes feelings of deception (Schweitzer et al., 2006). In that perspective, Ng and Feldman (2012) have shown that promises of future i-deals may be perceived as not an act of repentance but rather they might exacerbate the negative outcomes following damage to the employment relationship. The loss of trust following damage may make employees feel skeptical or cynical about the organization's ability and willingness to repair damage and fulfill its promise in the future, such that employees "may view promises of future deals as just another way for the organization to stall or delay honoring its commitments even further" (Ng & Feldman, 2012, p. 1464). The authors validate this hypothesis when employees have low job alternatives and feel "locked in" to the employment relationship. When job alternatives abound, promises of future i-deals have no effect on the psychological contract breach–organizational commitment relationship.

Overall, the literature indicates that promises of future i-deals may be less effective in repairing relationships than existing fulfilled i-deals.

The history of i-deals

The nature of past relationships sheds important light on the reparatory effects of i-deals. According to cognitive consistency research (Fiske & Taylor, 1984; Greenwald, 1980), employees will act in ways that reinforce prior knowledge, beliefs, or attitudes. When individuals interpret events that occur in their working environment, they tend to refer to selective perception such that prior beliefs tend to be confirmed rather than disconfirmed. The process of cognitive consistency has been observed in the literature on relationship repair (e.g., Kramer, 1996), which finds that a good past relationship helps predict future reconciliation (Tomlinson et al., 2004), and in the literature on psychological contracts, which finds that employees who experience a psychological contract breach tend to closely monitor the fulfillment of the contract, resulting in new perceptions of contract breaches (Lo & Aryee, 2003), even in the context of a new employment relationship (Kim & Choi, 2010).

I-deals negotiated before damage to the employment relationship was noticed may be used as evidence in evaluating the effects of i-deals negotiated after the damage. The literature on i-deals acknowledges that i-deals foster good relationships, especially when they are related to particularistic resources. Hornung et al. (2008) and Ng and Feldman (2010) found that i-deals are positively related to organizational commitment, while Lee and Hui (2011) and Rousseau et al. (2009) established a positive link with the quality of the employment relationship. Therefore, if past i-deals have been fulfilled, the employee is likely to see i-deals as a way to establish a good employment relationship. Through the cognitive consistency process, future i-deals should be welcomed and seen as helping to restore the relationship. Given that past fulfilled i-deals create a history of strong bonds, the interpretation of damage should be seen as less negative and employees will be more tolerant of damage (Morrison & Robinson, 1997), considering that the organization was not willing to harm them (based on past evidence of support and favorable treatment) and is able to act in their favor.

Conversely, past i-deals that have been unfulfilled by the organization should foster perceptions that i-deals will not be fulfilled in the future either. In such circumstances, new i-deals are likely to exacerbate perceptions of "cheap talk" and "makeup," and may harm the relationship rather than restore it (Ng & Feldman, 2012).

Discussion

Relying on Dirks et al.'s (2009) framework about relationship repair, this chapter proposes three mechanisms or processes through which i-deals might repair a damaged relationship: the attributional, exchange balance, and perceived controllability processes. These mechanisms highlight that negotiating i-deals can be seen as a process that modifies perceptions of the employer's intentionality, develops feelings of social standing, restores justice perceptions, and introduces controllability over the employer's actions. These three mechanisms suggest that i-deals might offer real opportunities to counterbalance the effects of a transgression in the employment relationship.

We identified variables that may moderate the effects of i-deals on damaged relationship repairs: the content, initiator, timing, and history of i-deals. Even if they were presented here one by one, in practice these variables combine to favor (or hinder) employment relationship repair. For example, in Ng and Feldman (2012), it is unclear whether i-deals have a negative impact on the employment relationship because they were initiated by the employer or because they were not yet honored. We suspect that it is a combination of these two factors that frustrates the employees, making them cynical about promises of future i-deals from the employer. Future research might want to explore the complexities of the combination of all of these potential moderators.

The literature on trust and relationship repair suggests that contextual factors that increase perceived controllability over the employment relationship, such as i-deals, can restart cooperation and maintain the bond between the concerned parties when trust is lost (Guseva & Rona-Tas, 2001), but may not be appropriate to restore trust and develop social exchanges in the long term (Kim et al., 2009; Malhotra & Murnighan, 2002; Sitkin & Roth, 1993). This means that i-deal negotiation is important to protect the individual from the damage perceived in the relationship, but i-deals might be insufficient to restore a social exchange in the long term if they are not accompanied by more implicit and informal forms of exchange. It is likely that the i-deals' repairing effects are stronger when combined with other repairing tactics that foster the development of more informal forms of exchange (e.g., stronger support from the team or the supervisor, better leader-member exchange, and more recognition of contributions; Cropanzano & Mitchell, 2005), which would collectively reinforce the perception that the relationship is changing. Future research might also want to explore, on a more short-term scale, combinations of i-deals and signals of repentance from the employer, such as apologies for transgressions (Dirks, Kim, Ferrin, & Cooper, 2011; Tomlinson et al., 2004).

In discussing the role of i-deals in damaged relationships, we proceeded as if the employment relationship was either black or white, damaged or positive/repaired. In fact, given the complexity of the employment relationship, we expect many gray zones between those two extremes. The employment relationship is also multifaceted, enabling parties to experience the positive and negative facets simultaneously (Dirks et al., 2009). Lewicki, McAllister, and Bies (1998) were the first to develop a framework for addressing this ambiguity (in this case between trust and distrust) in the same relationship. Future research might want to explore how i-deals help to repair the relationship in certain respects but not in others and maintain ambivalence in the employee–employer relationship.

Finally, in examining the role of i-deals in damaged relationships, we neglected to explore the i-deal bargaining process. I-deals that emerge from this fundamental negotiation process between employee and employer can be viewed as socially constructed through mutual influence processes. Accordingly, we hope future research will develop a more comprehensive view of how this bargaining process unfolds. It could be interesting to explore the dynamics of accepting or rejecting i-deal requests in damaged employment relationships vs. in positive employment relationships.

Note

1 Sylvie Guerrero and Kathleen Bentein, University of Quebec at Montreal, Canada.
2 These arguments were already partly developed in Guerrero et al. (2014).

References

Anand, S., Vidyarthi, P.R., Liden, R.C., & Rousseau, D.M. (2010). Good citizens in poor-quality relationships: Idiosyncratic deals as a substitute for relationship quality. *Academy of Management Journal, 53*(5), 970–988.
Bottom, W.P., Gibson, K., Daniels, S.E., & Murnighan, J.K. (2002). When talk is not cheap: Substantive penance and expressions of intent in rebuilding cooperation. *Organization Science, 13*(5), 497–513.
Clark, K., & Sefton, M. (2001). The sequential prisoner's dilemma: Evidence on reciprocation. *Economic Journal, 111*(468), 51–68.
Cropanzano, R., & Mitchell, M.S. (2005). Social exchange theory: An interdisciplinary review. *Journal of Management, 31*(6), 874–900.
Dirks, K.T., Kim, P.H., Ferrin, D.L., & Cooper, C.D. (2011). Understanding the effects of substantive responses on trust following a transgression. *Organizational Behavior and Human Decision Processes, 114*, 87–103.
Dirks, K.T., Lewicki, R.J., & Zaheer, A. (2009). Repairing relationships within and between organizations: Building a conceptual foundation. *Academy of Management Review, 34*(1), 68–84.
Farrell, D. (1983). Exit, voice, loyalty and neglect as responses to job dissatisfaction: A multi-dimensional scaling study. *Academy of Management Journal, 26*, 596–607.
Farrell, J., & Gibbons, R.S. (1989). Cheap talk can matter in bargaining. *Journal of Economic Theory, 48*, 221–37.
Ferrin, D.L., Kim, P.H., Cooper, C.D., & Dirks, K.T. (2007). Silence speaks volumes: The effectiveness of reticence in comparison to apology and denial for responding to integrity- and competence-based trust violations. *Journal of Applied Psychology, 92*(4), 893–908.
Fiske, S.T., & Taylor, S.E. (1984). *Social cognition.* New York: Random House.
Foa, U.G., & Foa, E.B. (1975). *Societal structures of the mind.* Springfield, IL: Thomas.
Gibson, K., Bottom, W., & Murnighan, J.K. (1999). Once bitten: Defection and reconciliation in a cooperative enterprise. *Business Ethics Quarterly, 9*(1), 69–85.
Goffman, E. (1967). *Interaction ritual: Essays on face-to-face behavior.* Garden City, NY: Anchor Books.
Goldman, B.M., Gutek, B.A., Stein, J.H., & Lewis, K. (2006). Employment discrimination in organizations: Antecedents and consequences. *Journal of Management, 32*(6), 786–830.
Greenwald, A.G. (1980). The totalitarian ego: Fabrication and revision of personal history. *American Psychologist, 35*, 603–618.
Guerrero, S., Bentein, K., & Lapalme, M-È. (2014). Idiosyncratic deals and high-performers' organizational commitment. *Journal of Business and Psychology, 29*(2), 323–334.
Guseva, A., & Rona-Tas, A. (2001). Uncertainty, risk and trust: Russian and American credit card markets compared. *American Sociological Review, 66*, 623–646.
Heider, F. (1958). *The psychology of interpersonal relations.* New York: Wiley.
Hirschman, A.O. (1970). *Exit, voice, and loyalty: Responses to decline in firms, organizations, and states.* Cambridge, MA: Harvard University Press.
Hornung, S., Glaser, J., & Rousseau, D.M. (2010a). Interdependence as an i(-)deal: Enhancing job autonomy and distributive justice via individual negotiation. *German Journal of Research in Human Resource Management, 24*(2), 108–129.

Hornung, S., Rousseau, D.M., & Glaser, J. (2008). Creating flexible work arrangements through idiosyncratic deals. *Journal of Applied Psychology, 93*(3), 655–664.

Hornung, S., Rousseau, D.M., & Glaser, J. (2009). Why supervisors make idiosyncratic deals: Antecedents and outcomes of i-deals from a managerial perspective. *Journal of Managerial Psychology, 24*(8), 738–764.

Hornung, S., Rousseau, D.M., Glaser, J., Angerer, P., & Weigl, M. (2010b). Beyond top-down and bottom-up work redesign: Customizing job content through idiosyncratic deals. *Journal of Organizational Behavior, 31*, 187–215.

Kim, M.S., & Choi, J.N. (2010). Layoff victims' employment relationship with a new employer in Korea: Effects of unmet tenure expectations on trust and psychological contract. *International Journal of Human Resource Management, 21*, 781–798.

Kim, P.H., Dirks, K.T., & Cooper, C.D. (2009). The repair of trust: A dynamic bilateral perspective and multilevel conceptualization. *Academy of Management Review, 34*(3), 401–422.

Kim, P.H., Dirks, K.T., Cooper, C.D., & Ferrin, D.L. (2006). When more blame is better than less: The implications of internal vs. external attributions for the repair of trust after a competence- vs. integrity-based trust violation. *Organizational Behavior and Human Decision Processes, 99*, 49–65.

Kim, P.H., Ferrin, D.L., Cooper, C.D., & Dirks, K.T. (2004). Removing the shadow of suspicion: The effects of apology vs. denial for repairing ability- vs. integrity-based trust violations. *Journal of Applied Psychology, 89*(1), 104–118.

Kramer, R.M. (1996). Divergent realities and convergent disappointments in the hierarchic relation: Trust and the intuitive auditor at work. In R.M. Kramer & T.R. Tyler (Eds.), *Trust in organizations: Frontiers of theory and research* (pp. 216–245). Thousand Oaks, CA: Sage.

Labianca, G., Brass, D.J., & Gray, B. (1998). Social networks and perceptions of intergroup conflict: The role of negative relationships and third parties. *Academy of Management Journal, 41*(1), 55–67.

Lee, C., & Hui, C. (2011). Antecedents and consequences of idiosyncratic deals: A frame of resource exchange. *Frontiers of Business Research in China, 5*(3), 380–401.

Lewicki, R.J., McAllister, D.J., & Bies, R.J. (1998). Trust and distrust: New relationships and realities. *Academy of Management Review, 23*, 438–458.

Liu, J., Lee, C., Hui, C., Kwan, H.K., & Wu, L.-Z. (2013). Idiosyncratic deals and employee outcomes: The mediating roles of social exchange and self-enhancement and the moderating role of individualism. *Journal of Applied Psychology, 98*(5), 832–840.

Lo, S., & Aryee, S. (2003). Psychological contract breach in a Chinese context: An integrative approach. *Journal of Management Studies, 40*, 1005–1020.

Malhotra, D., & Murnighan, J.K. (2002). The effects of contracts on interpersonal trust. *Administrative Science Quarterly, 47*, 534–559.

Mayer, R.C., Davis, J.H., & Schoorman, F.D. (1995). An integrative model of organizational trust. *Academy of Management Review, 20*(3), 709–734.

Molm, T., Takahashi, N., & Peterson, G. (2000). Risk and trust in social exchange: An experimental test of a classic proposition. *American Journal of Sociology, 105*, 1396–1427.

Morrison, E.W., & Robinson, S.L. (1997). When employees feel betrayed: A model of how psychological contract violation develops. *Academy of Management Review, 22*, 226–256.

Ng, T.W., & Feldman, D.C. (2010). Idiosyncratic deals and organizational commitment. *Journal of Vocational Behavior, 76*, 419–427.

Ng, T.W.H., & Feldman, D.C. (2012). Breaches of past promises, current job alternatives, and promises of future idiosyncratic deals: Three-way interaction effects on organizational commitment. *Human Relations, 65*(11), 1463–1486.

Robinson, S.L. (1996). Trust and breach of the psychological contract. *Administrative Science Quarterly, 41*(4), 574–599.

Rousseau, D.M. (2005). *I-deals: Idiosyncratic deals employees bargain for themselves.* Armonk, NY: M.E. Sharpe.

Rousseau, D.M., Ho, V.T., & Greenberg, J. (2006). I-deals: Idiosyncratic terms in employment relationships. *Academy of Management Review, 31*(4), 977–994.

Rousseau, D.M., Hornung, S., & Kim, T.G. (2009). Idiosyncratic deals: Testing propositions on timing, content, and the employment relationship. *Journal of Vocational Behavior, 74,* 338–348.

Schweitzer, M.E., Hershey, J.C., & Bradlow, E.T. (2006). Promises and lies: Restoring violated trust. *Organizational Behavior and Human Decision Processes, 101*(1), 1–19.

Sitkin, S.B., & Roth, N.L. (1993). Explaining the limited effectiveness of legalistic "remedies" for trust/distrust. *Organization Science, 4,* 367–392.

Tomlinson, E.C., Dineen, B.R., & Lewicki, R.J. (2004). The road to reconciliation: Antecedents of victim willingness to reconcile following a broken promise. *Journal of Management, 30,* 165–187.

Tomlinson, E.C., & Mayer, R.C. (2009). The role of causal attribution dimensions in trust repair. *Academy of Management Review, 34*(1), 85–104.

Turnley, W.H., & Feldman, D.C. (1999). The impact of psychological contract violations on exit, voice, loyalty, and neglect. *Human Relations, 52*(7), 895–922.

Weiner, B. (1986). *An attributional theory of motivation and emotion.* New York: Springer Verlag.

4
NOT SO I-DEAL

A critical review of idiosyncratic deals theory and research

Neil Conway and Jacqueline Coyle-Shapiro[1]

Introduction

The notion that some employees cut special deals with their employers in order to advance their own interests will strike a chord with most people. We may know of occasions when we have made such arrangements; more likely, we may suspect others in our workplace have such arrangements. Furthermore, i-deals fit with some evidence and management discourse about the increasing individualization of the employment relationship and proliferation of different types of employment contracts (Bidwell, Briscoe, Fernandez-Mateo, & Sterling, 2013).

We put the concept of i-deals under the microscope and critically review its definition, theory, and empirical evidence with the motivation of provoking debate about this intriguing idea. We begin by briefly reviewing the current state of i-deals research and then gauge the extent to which it has captured researchers' interest. We highlight confusing aspects of the i-deals definition and critique its features. Following this, we assess the offered theoretical mechanisms linking i-deals to putative outcomes and consider whether i-deals offer a novel lens to understand the employee–organization relationship. Finally, we identify problems with the ways i-deals have been measured and raise issues about the research designs used in empirical studies.

Current state of i-deals research

"I-deals refer to voluntary, personalized agreements of a nonstandard nature negotiated between individual employees and their employers regarding terms that benefit each party" (Rousseau, Ho, & Greenberg, 2006, p. 978). The distinguishing features of i-deals are that they are individually negotiated by either the employer or the employee, heterogeneous in that some of the terms are differentiated from what other comparable employees receive, mutually beneficial so that both the interests of the employee and employer are served, and vary in scope from a single idiosyncratic element to an entirely different deal (Rousseau, 2005; Rousseau et al., 2006). Researchers argue that organizations use i-deals to recruit, retain, and reward high performers; for employees, i-deals can signal their market value or the value an employer places on the individual employee (Rosen, Slater, Chang, & Johnson, 2013; Rousseau, 2005; Rousseau et al., 2006).

So, what does the empirical evidence reveal? Table 4.1 provides an overview of the fifteen published empirical articles (a few of the articles contain multiple studies) on i-deals in terms of definition, dimensions, outcomes, moderators, design, findings, and sample. A noticeable feature is the variation in definitions of i-deals used by researchers. Definitions commonly include employees negotiating a special employment arrangement (not on offer to other employees) with their employer. Beyond this, the definitions diverge: some for instance focus on the benefit to both the employee and employer (e.g., Lai, Rousseau, & Chang, 2009), while others are more employee focused in highlighting the satisfaction of specific personal preferences and needs of the employee (e.g., Ng & Feldman, 2012b).

The definitions also indicate that i-deals can cover a single idiosyncratic element to a completely different "deal" involving many different terms. However, researchers tend to operationalize i-deals as having a small number of dimensions, elements, or terms. Studies differ in terms of the range of dimensions and which dimensions are captured. For example, Anand et al. (2010) focus on one dimension, developmental i-deals; Bal et al. (2012) include developmental and flexibility i-deals; Hornung et al. (2008) capture three dimensions: developmental, flexibility, and workload reduction i-deals; Rosen et al. (2013) capture four dimensions: schedule flexibility, task and work responsibilities, location flexibility, and financial incentives; finally, Ng and Feldman (2010) draw on six elements to capture i-deals.

Most studies consider whether employees' self-reports of i-deals are associated with self-reported outcomes. I-deals have been linked to a wide range of outcomes, including affective commitment, work–family conflict/balance, work engagement, voice, proactive behaviors, motivation to continue working, working overtime, citizenship behaviors, and employee performance. Five studies consider factors that may moderate associations between i-deals and proposed outcomes (e.g., Bal, De Jong, Jansen, & Bakker, 2012).

With such a variety of outcome variables, it is difficult to discern a pattern in the findings. A recent meta-analysis pulls together the findings of 23 published and unpublished studies across Western (i.e., Germany, the United States, and the Netherlands) and Eastern (i.e., China, India, and South Korea) cultures, and suggests some consistency across studies, where i-deals were significantly negatively related to turnover intentions and positively related to job satisfaction (in Western and Eastern cultures) and affective commitment (in Eastern cultures) (Liao, Wayne, & Rousseau, 2014). However, tempering confidence in the positive effects of i-deals, it should be noted that the effect sizes were small (ranging from .09 to .25), based on small numbers of samples (ranging from 2 to 5), and the findings were somewhat

TABLE 4.1 An Overview of I-Deals Definitions, Methods, and Findings

Study	Definition	Dimensions	Example item
Hornung, S., Rousseau, D.M., & Glaser, J. (2008)	Idiosyncratic deals ("i-deals"), where individual employees negotiate with an employer to adapt work arrangements to better meet their personal needs (Rousseau, 2005).... I-deals are a form of customization granting employees special conditions differing from peers doing similar work. Not limited to freelancers (Pink, 2002) or stars (Rosen, 1981), regular employees also seek out and bargain for special employment conditions that satisfy their personal needs and preferences.	2 dimensions: Flexibility and Development	Hornung et al. (2008) measure: Respondents rated the extent to which they had "asked for and successfully negotiated individual arrangements different from their peers in terms of flexibility and development"... "flexibility in starting and ending the working day"
Hornung, S., Rousseau, D.M., & Glaser, J. (2009)	I-deals are special terms of employment, negotiated by individual workers and authorized by agents of their employers (e.g., supervisors, higher-level managers, human resource representatives; Rousseau, 2001, 2004, 2005).	3 dimensions: Flexibility, Development, and Workload reduction	Adapted from Rousseau and Kim (2006): to what extent have you (the supervisor) authorized special flexibility in working hours?
Lai, L., Rousseau, D.M., & Chang, K.T.T. (2009)	Idiosyncratic deals (i-deals for short) are personalized employment arrangements negotiated between individual workers and employers	General item	"the kinds of requests that individual workers make to their employer to obtain atypical or nonstandard employment arrangements. These requests cover a host of issues from working conditions (e.g., schedule, working at home), development opportunities

Outcomes	Moderators	Design	Findings	Sample
Work–family conflict, performance expectations, overtime hours worked, affective commitment	None	Cross-sectional	Work arrangements and personal initiative predicted i-deal negotiation; Developmental i-deals positively related to affective commitment, work-family conflict, performance expectations, and overtime; Flexibility i-deals negatively related to work–family conflict and overtime	887 public sector employees
Supervisors' rating of change in performance, motivation, and Work–Life balance of employees	None	Cross-sectional	Employee initiative associated with authorization of developmental and flexibility i-deals; Unfulfilled obligations positively associated with workload reduction i-deals; Developmental ideals associated with increased performance, changes in employee motivation; Flexibility i-deals associated with changes in work–life balance.	Same study as above with 263 supervisors
Acceptance of another's i-deal	None	Cross-sectional network analysis	More likely to accept another's i-deal when the other is a close friend, when you believe a similar deal may be offered to you in the future, and when you have a social exchange	US high-tech firm, 65 employees from 20 teams

(Continued)

TABLE 4.1. (Continued)

Study	Definition	Dimensions	Example item
	and intended to benefit them both (Rousseau, 2001).		(e.g., special training, assignments) as well as other benefits." ... "If your coworkers ask for special individual arrangements in the near future, to what extent would you be willing to accept them having arrangements different from your own?"
Rousseau, D.M., Hornung, S., & Kim, T. G (2009)	I-deals are personalized agreements of a nonstandard nature; individual employees seek out and negotiate with their employer	2 dimensions: Work hours and Developmental	Extent to which participant had asked for and successfully negotiated a schedule different from coworkers
Anand, S., Vidyarthi, P.R., Liden, R.C., & Rousseau, D.M. (2010)	Idiosyncratic deals (i-deals) are individually bargained employment arrangements intended to benefit both worker and organization. I-deals are not individuals' subjective understandings, as are "psychological contracts" (worker beliefs regarding exchange relationships in employment). Rather, they are objective conditions that employees negotiate with an employer to enhance their employment arrangements.	1 dimension: Developmental	"Supervisors were asked if an employee had 'training opportunities,' 'skill development opportunities,' 'on-the-job activities,' and 'career development opportunities' that were 'different from his/her coworkers'"

Outcomes	Moderators	Design	Findings	Sample
			relationship with your employer, and less likely to be accepting when you have economic exchange.	
Social exchange (SE) and economic exchange (EE)	None	Cross sectional T1 and T2 data	Ex post negotiation positive related to SE and negatively related to EE; Developmental i-deals positively related to SE; Work hour i-deals negatively related to SE; Developmental i-deals negatively related and work hour i-deals positively related to EE	145 and 120 hospital employees
Organizational citizenship behaviors to individuals (OCBI), organizational citizenship behaviors to organization (OCBO)	Leader-member exchange (LMX), perceived organizational support (POS)	Cross-sectional	I-deals positively related to OCBO and OCBI; Relationship between i-deals and OCBO and OCBI stronger when LMX low; Relationship between i-deals and OCBO stronger when team-member exchange (TMX) low; No moderating effect of POS. I-deals have no effect in high-quality relationships, but are effective in low-quality relationships	246 matched employee–manager dyads in software industry (only supervisors reported on i-deals)

(*Continued*)

TABLE 4.1. (Continued)

Study	Definition	Dimensions	Example item
Hornung, S., Rousseau, D.M., Glaser, J., Angerer, P., & Weigl, M. (2010)	Idiosyncratic deals, in general, are employment terms individuals negotiate for themselves, taking myriad forms from flexible schedules to career development (Rousseau, 2001, 2005).	1 dimension: Task related	Based on Hornung et al. (2008) and Rousseau and Kim (2006): Respondents rated the extent to which they had "asked for and successfully negotiated personalized conditions in their current job, e.g., special job duties or assignments, work tasks that suit my personal interest"
Ng, T.W.H., & Feldman, D. C (2010)	Idiosyncratic contracts are employment arrangements that are different in nature from those given to other employees and are crafted to meet the specific needs of individual employees. These idiosyncratic contracts offer employees additional resources (e.g., special promotion tracks or flexible scheduling) not readily available to their colleagues (Rousseau, Ho, & Greenberg, 2006)	6 elements: Pay, Advancement opportunities, Training, Career development, Job security, Support with personal problems	"This organization provides me with a level of pay that most employees in my team/unit do not get"
Hornung, S., Rousseau, D.M., Glaser, J., Angerer, P., & Weigl, M. (2011)	Idiosyncratic deals (called "i-deals" by some authors) are personalized arrangements workers negotiate with their employer to make their jobs more supportive of their individual needs, preferences, and aspirations (Rousseau, 2001, 2005; Rousseau, Ho, & Greenberg, 2006).... idiosyncratic deals have been	2 dimensions: Flexibility and Developmental	Hornung et al. (2008) measure: Respondents rated the extent to which they had "negotiated personalized working conditions deviating from applicable standards on a 5-point scale" in terms of flexibility and development ..."more influence over working hours"

Outcomes	Moderators	Design	Findings	Sample
Task complexity, Task control, Stressors, Work Engagement, Personal Initiative	None	Cross-sectional	LMX associated with task i-deals; Task i-deals positively associated with complexity and control and negatively with stressors that in turn associated negatively with work engagement	Employee samples from hospitals in US (N=207) and Germany (N=292)
Affective Commitment (AC)	Core self-evaluations (CSE), Age	Cross lagged: IV at T1 and DV at T2	I-contracts positively linked to AC; relationship stronger for low CSE (no support for age as moderator) and strongest relationship between i-contracts and AC for individuals low in CSE and who were older (chronologically and subjectively)	375 US managers across organizations
Work–family conflict, Work engagement	None	Cross-lagged	Leader consideration positively related to i-deals; Developmental i-deals predicted work engagement; Flexibility i-deals negatively predicted work family conflict; Mediating effect of i-deals in relationship between leader consideration and work engagement/work–family conflict	159 at T1 and 142 at T2 hospital physicians used in prior study

(Continued)

TABLE 4.1. (Continued)

Study	Definition	Dimensions	Example item
	suggested to be mutually beneficial for employees and employers by increasing the fit between the person and the job and thereby providing conditions which support the worker's well-being and sustained performance.		
Lee, C., & Hui, C. (2011)	Idiosyncratic deals refer to the special conditions that individual workers bargain for, and that differ from the standards applying to their peers	3 dimensions: Personal development, Flexibility, and Reduced workload	Rousseau and Kim (2006)

Outcomes	Moderators	Design	Findings	Sample
Psychological contracts: Relational, balanced, and transactional	None	Cross lagged (6 weeks): I-deals at T1 and DV at time 2	Individualism positively related to ex ante but not ex post i-deals; Social skills positively related to ex ante and ex post i-deals; Perceived insider status positively related to ex post i-deals; Ex ante i-deals more positively related to transactional psychological contracts than ex post i-deals; Ex post i-deals more positively related to relational and balanced psychological contracts than ex ante; Personal development i-deals more positively related to relational and balanced psychological contracts; Flexibility and workload reduction i-deals relate more positively to transactional psychological contracts	289 telecommunications employees in China

(Continued)

TABLE 4.1. (Continued)

Study	Definition	Dimensions	Example item
Bal, P.M., De Jong, S.B., Jansen, P.G., & Bakker, A.B. (2012)	I-deals are defined as "voluntary, personalized agreements of a nonstandard nature negotiated between individual employees and their employers regarding terms that benefit each party" (Rousseau et al., 2006, p. 978)	2 dimensions: Flexibility and Developmental	Hornung et al. (2008) measure: Respondents rated the extent to which they had "asked for and successfully negotiated individual arrangements different from their peers" in terms of flexibility and development "flexibility in starting and ending the working day" and "training opportunities"
Ng, T.W.H., & Feldman, D. C (2012a)	Future i-deals (Rousseau et al., 2006) and contract idiosyncrasy. Difference is "research on i-deals has examined how employees react to i-deals after they have been honored (or not). Contract idiosyncrasy has focused on how employees react to promises of future i-deals before they have been honored"	6 elements: Pay, Advancement opportunities, Training, Career development, Job security, Support with personal problems	"This organization promises me a level of pay that most employees in my team/unit dc not get"

Outcomes	Moderators	Design	Findings	Sample
Motivation to continue working after retirement age	Accommodative and development climate	Cross-sectional	Flexibility i-deals but not developmental i-deals positively associated with motivation to continue working; Accommodative climate moderated the relationship between developmental i-deals and motivation to continue working and development climate moderated the relationship between development i-deals and motivation to continue working	Employees in two healthcare organizations; 24 units, $N = 1083$
Affective Commitment	Future i-deals, perceived job alternatives	Cross lagged: IV at T1 and DV at T2	Breach of past promises negatively related to AC; No moderating effect of future i-deals on relationship between breach and AC; Negative relationship between breach and AC is strongest when future i-deals promised and few job alternatives. Item level analysis – effect size of three-way interaction strongest for support for personal problems, job security, pay and skill training. Weakest for career development and advancement opportunities	196 across range of industries

(Continued)

TABLE 4.1. (Continued)

Study	Definition	Dimensions	Example item
Ng, T.W.H., & Feldman, D. C. (2012b)	I-deals – special employment arrangements that are tailored to the personal preferences and needs of employees	2 Dimensions: Flexibility and Professional development	Hornung et al. (2008) "I asked for and successfully negotiated individual arrangements different from my peers in terms of flexibility in starting and ending the workday"
Liu, J., Lee, C., Hui, C., Kwan, H.K., & Wu, L.Z. (2013)	Employees increasingly negotiate idiosyncratic deals ("i-deals"), that is, customized work arrangements, with their employers (Rousseau, 2005).	2 Dimensions: Flexibility and Developmental	Rousseau and Kim (2006)

Outcomes	Moderators	Design	Findings	Sample
Constructive voice	None. Mediators: flexible work role orientation, networking behavior and organizational trust	Longitudinal; IVs and DVs measured on three measurement occasions over 10 months	Flexibility i-deals associated with voice behavior in China but not US sample. Professional development i-deals associated with voice behavior. Support for mediating role of flexible work orientation in the professional development i-deals and voice relationship in Chinese sample. Networking behavior mediates i-deals – voice relationship in both samples. Organizational trust mediates relationship between scheduling flexibility i-deals and voice in both samples but found to mediate the relationship between professional development i-deals and voice in Chinese sample only. Stronger mediating role of flexible work role orientation, social networking behavior and organizational trust found in China than US.	265 US and 201 Chinese managers
Organization-based self-esteem (OBSE), POS, Proactive Behaviors, Affective Commitment	Individualism	Cross Lagged: IVs at Time 1, mediators Time 2, and DVs at Time 3	POS mediates relationship between i-deals and AC and proactive behaviors; OBSE mediates the relationship between i-deals and AC and proactive behaviors; OBSE's mediation significant for high individualism and mediation of POS significant for low individualism	230 employee and 102 supervisors from 2 Chinese organizations

(Continued)

TABLE 4.1. (Continued)

Study	Definition	Dimensions	Example item
Rosen, C.C., Slater, D.J., Chang, C.-H., Johnson, R.E. (2013)	I-deals: "voluntary, personalized agreements of a nonstandard nature negotiated between individual employers and employees regarding terms that benefit each party"	4 dimensions: Schedule flexibility, Task and work responsibilities, Location flexibility, Financial incentives	"Because of my personal circumstances, my supervisor has created a compensation arrangement that is tailored to fit me." 16-item scale capturing 4 dimensions
Vidyarthi, Chaudhry, A., Anand, S., & Liden, B. C. (2014)	I-deals defined as personalized employment arrangements negotiated between individual workers and employers intended to benefit both parties	1 dimension: Flexibility i-deals	Managers were asked, "Is this employee given flexibility in starting and ending his/her work day?"

Outcomes	Moderators	Design	Findings	Sample
Organizational Commitment (OC) Job Satisfaction (JS)	None	Longitudinal (10 weeks): I-deals at T1 and T2, DVs at time 2	Study 3: Task and work responsibility i-deals positively related to JS and all types of OC; Financial incentives i-deals linked to continuance OC; Schedule flexibility i-deals linked to job satisfaction	Study 3: 280 employed undergrad students
	None	Longitudinal (5 weeks): I-deals at T1 and T2, DVs at time 2	Study 4: Task and work responsibility i-deals positively related to JS and all types of OC except continuance OC; Schedule flexibility i-deals linked to JS, affective OC, and continuance OC; Financial incentives i-deals and location flexibility i-deals not related to job satisfaction and OC	Study 4: 196 working adults
POS and Career satisfaction	None	Cross sectional	U-shaped relationship between flexibility i-deals and POS and career satisfaction – high POS and career satisfaction found at low and high levels of flexibility i-deals	207 supervisor–subordinate dyads of computer engineers in India

inconsistent in that i-deals did not relate significantly to affective commitment in Western cultures (based on aggregated findings from 5 samples).

Research designs used to examine i-deals tend to offer weak forms of evidence. The majority of i-deals studies are cross-sectional or separate the measurement of the independent and dependent variables. In the minority are longitudinal studies used with repeated measures of the independent and dependent variables (see for example, Ng & Feldman, 2012b; Rosen et al., 2013). In general, the stronger the research design, the weaker the support for the effects of i-deals, and therefore findings based on weak methods may exaggerate support for i-deals (note this is based on only a small number of repeated measures studies). For instance, Hornung et al.'s (2011) longitudinal findings are less supportive than other studies based on cross-sectional findings (cf. Hornung et al., 2008) in terms of failing to find lagged associations between i-deals and expected outcomes (a nonsignificant lagged association between flexibility i-deals and work–family conflict), and also finding lagged associations that question the assumed direction of causality between i-deals and outcomes (significant reciprocal associations between developmental i-deals and work engagement). Elsewhere, longitudinal findings indicate changes to i-deals vary alongside changes in the outcomes of social networking and organizational trust (Ng & Feldman, 2012b), providing stronger evidence of covariation than cross-sectional designs but not providing insight into the direction of causality.

In summary, the empirical studies offer some support for associations between i-deals and outcomes; however, the effects of i-deals are small and somewhat mixed. Against this backdrop, we now begin our critical review, considering first whether i-deals have energized research activity.

Researcher interest in i-deals

I-deals researchers typically claim that it is an area of great interest and attention, being a "topic of considerable research" (Anand et al., 2010, p. 970), and one that has received "considerable attention as a means of building organizational commitment" (Ng & Feldman, 2012b, p. 1). However, the level of interest is belied by the small number of available empirical articles (as Table 1 indicates), and indeed researchers acknowledge that there have been "few empirical studies" (Ng & Feldman, 2012b, p. 2).

To gain some indication of the extent of i-deals research activity since its introduction, we searched for i-deals journal articles in *Business Source Complete*, a popular and comprehensive database of scholarly business journals. We took Rousseau's 2005 book on i-deals as introducing the i-deals concept, although we note Rousseau's 2001 article in *Organizational Dynamics* and some precursor studies cited by i-deals researchers (such as Lawler & Finegold, 2000; Miner, 1987). Since 2005 and over the last 9 years, only 21 articles include the term "i-deals" or "idiosyncratic deals" in the abstract of scholarly peer-reviewed journal articles (as of November 17, 2014). Furthermore, and as Table 1 reveals, Rousseau and her collaborators author 7 of these 21 articles.

To place this level of research activity in context, we compared it to research activity on the psychological contract during the nine-year period after Rousseau's 1989 reconceptualization of the psychological contract, which was widely regarded as reinvigorating psychological contract research (Conway & Briner, 2005). Comparing i-deals with the psychological contract makes some sense, as both concepts and related theories were generated by Rousseau, both are often portrayed as rooted in social exchange, and both were presented as examples of a trend in the individualization of the employment relationship. During the nine-year period between 1989 and 1998, a search in *Business Source Complete* shows 63 articles include the term "psychological contract" in the abstract of scholarly journal articles.

From this crude analysis, we conclude that researchers have shown lukewarm interest in i-deals since its introduction, in both absolute and relative terms, and there is little indication as yet of it being an area of current major interest. Indeed, we may well ponder: why the lack of interest? Potential explanations for the low uptake may be that the idea lacks a precise definition, clear theoretical mechanisms linking it to outcomes, and unique value beyond existing ideas. To these matters we now turn.

I-deals definitions lack clarity, precision, and consistency

As we can see from Table 1, i-deals definitions have some common features (Rousseau et al., 2006), and in this section we focus on three features that follow clearly from inspecting the definitions: I-deals are (a) individually explicitly negotiated; (b) beneficial to parties; and (c) nonstandard, idiosyncratic bargains that range in scope of content and vary across employees. In this section, we highlight some critical inconsistencies and ambiguities across definitions.

To what extent are i-deals explicitly negotiated?

It is currently unclear whether i-deals result from explicit negotiation with another party or arise from more implicit negotiations. Some i-deals definitions clearly emphasize that they refer to explicit and objective agreements where, for instance, Anand and colleagues state that "i-deals are not individuals' subjective understandings, as are psychological contracts . . . rather, they are objective conditions that employees negotiate with an employer" (Anand et al., 2010, p. 970). Elsewhere in i-deals research, it is defined and referred to in a way that emphasizes more implicit processes. For instance Ng and Feldman (2010, p. 420) refer to employment "arrangements" which are "crafted" to meet the needs of employees; i-deals are likely to be construed as "special gestures" (Anand et al., 2010, p. 972). Furthermore, most i-deals research uses social exchange as the theoretical foundation of i-deals (Rosen et al., 2013), where social exchanges consist of unspecified obligations that can be short or long term and open-ended. This implicit nature is illustrated, for example, when researchers argue that following successful negotiation of i-deals, employees are "*likely* to feel obligated to those who granted or enabled their deals"

(Anand et al., 2010, p. 972, italics added). Therefore, even if the initial i-deals negotiation of what the employee gets tends toward explicitness, what the employee is expected to do in return is assumed to follow a social exchange process, where organizations expect obligations to be discharged, but do not know when or how. In other words, whether employees reciprocate may well be highly implicit.

Related to the explicit or implicit nature of i-deals is whether they are made public or held at a private level. I-deals literature tends to state that it is desirable for i-deals to be made public; however, in most cases this will not be the case: "Coworkers may view i-deals positively if their visibility or public nature makes them appear normative. In most firms, i-deals are not public, instead taking the form of informal, private arrangements" (Lai et al., 2009, p. 553). The language of informal, private arrangements is much closer to an implicitly negotiated deal than one that is explicitly objective, and such i-deals will certainly be viewed as implicit by third-party coworkers who may speculate about the fairness of employees receiving i-deals and be concerned that favoritism is taking place.

In summary, the implicit aspects of i-deals are unclear. The extent to which i-deals are explicitly or implicitly negotiated is important because if it is implicit, then i-deals become indiscriminate to psychological contracts and i-deals should therefore be viewed as much more subjectively understood by employees. If i-deals are highly subjective, then individuals may have a sense of receiving a beneficial deal, but cannot be sure of its benefits because it is implicit and they will be unaware of other employees' implicit i-deals. As an implicit phenomenon, perhaps i-deals will not satisfy "star" employees who seek demonstrable, objective indicators of their value to the organization that clearly distinguish them apart from their peers. From an organization's perspective, if i-deals are a highly implicit phenomenon, then it will not benefit organizations that wish to use i-deals as a means of communicating or signaling an equity-based culture where the most-valued employees are duly rewarded. To conclude, the extent to which i-deals are implicit is unclear; if they are highly implicit, then the concept of i-deals risks being indistinct to psychological contracts and its value to organizations as a signaling mechanism is greatly reduced.

Do i-deals benefit one or both parties?

It is currently unclear whether i-deals are mutually beneficial to both employees and the organization, or beneficial to only one party, or indeed involve costs to one or both parties. There is inconsistency between the definitions used by researchers as to whether i-deals are mutually beneficial (or not). On the one hand, the definitions used by Rousseau and colleagues and Bal and colleagues clearly stress that i-deals are intended to benefit both the worker and organization negotiating the i-deal (e.g., in Table 1, see definitions by Anand et al., 2010; Hornung et al., 2011; Lai et al., 2009, etc.). On the other hand, definitions, particularly those arising from Ng and Feldman (2010, 2012a, 2012b) emphasize the benefit to employees but do not emphasize employer benefits (e.g., i-deals are "crafted to meet the specific needs of individual employees," Ng & Feldman, 2010, p. 420). Indeed, Ng and Feldman go further to state that "practically speaking, idiosyncratic deals are costly to organizations" (Ng & Feldman, 2010, p. 219), which is clearly evident when i-deals involve lucrative compensation packages. Even advocates of the mutual benefits of i-deals somewhat understatedly acknowledge the costs to organizations, where "an i-deal granting supervisor may tolerate some inconvenience to promote an i-deal" (Anand et al., 2010, p. 972).

I-deals research is also unclear about when organizations expect to accrue the benefits of i-deals. Are the benefits to organizations clear and objective at the point of negotiating the i-deal, or are the benefits more a reference to the hoped-for longer term effects of the i-deal that are assumed to materialize through a social exchange reciprocation process at some unspecified future time point? The i-deals literature tends to assume that the benefits of i-deals from an organization's perspective accrue via social exchange processes, where employees receiving an i-deal feel obliged to reciprocate. However, as we noted above, obligations arising from social exchanges are only likely to be discharged at an unknown future time point (Rosen et al., 2013), and therefore when do organizations become aware of the benefits, if at all? If there are doubts about when the intended benefits to the organization will arise, or if benefits will arise at all, can it still be considered an i-deal?

More clearly establishing who benefits from i-deals is important for several reasons. First, mutual benefits are seen as the key factor differentiating i-deals from favoritism: "I-deals differ from favouritism because they are intended to benefit not only their recipient but also the recipients' organization" (Anand et al., 2010, p. 972). Note, however, that Rousseau et al. (2006, p. 980) acknowledge that the distinction between i-deals and favoritism is a "gray area" in some instances. In other words, the case for the benefits of i-deals can appear to argue for the benefits of favoritism, which is likely to be unpalatable in most workplaces.

Second, the ambiguity about whether i-deals are intended to benefit just the employee or to the organization as well casts doubt on our ability to identify i-deals. For instance, if an i-deal benefits only one party, is it still an i-deal? If it is beneficial to only one party, how is it to the other party – neutral, or potentially costly? And if we allow i-deals to benefit only one party and are agnostic as to how it affects the other party, then can organizations benefit at the cost to an employee? For instance, i-deals could be interpreted as having a "dark side" where organizations single out and make an example of an underperforming employee. This may benefit the organization and be idiosyncratic, but it is not to the employee's benefit. Third, the idea that i-deals are mutually beneficial is a nice fantasy, but such win-win deals are unlikely in real life. Social exchanges entail give and take, and even if there are some benefits to each party, there will also be costs. This aspect of i-deals is rarely considered. For example, do parties to an i-deal benefit on each and every term of the arrangement, or on some terms but not others?

Clarifying the contents and recipients of the nonstandard, idiosyncratic bargain in i-deals

Two interconnected issues about clarifying the scope of the contents of i-deals (i.e., the terms) and scope of recipients (i.e., who is eligible for i-deals) are troubling.

Regarding the scope of i-deals, the contents are acknowledged as very wide ranging, for example: "I-deals vary in content and scope from a single feature to the entire set of conditions composing the employment relationship, ranging from minor adjustments in hours or duties to highly customized" (Hornung et al., 2008, p. 656). I-deals, therefore, can be about anything and everything.

Turning to who are the likely recipients of i-deals, the literature is unclear as to how widely available they are to employees. Some i-deals literature suggests they are reserved for "stars" and "highly valued employees" (Rosen et al., 2013, p. 710), who will be "particularly excited about being the only one (or one of a few) to receive rare and valued resources" (Ng & Feldman, 2010, p. 420). However, other literature presents the offering of i-deals as a much more routine and widespread happening (such as Anand et al., 2010), and indeed the fact that i-deals can range so widely across terms of an employment relationship suggests they are in theory widely available.

The routine and widespread contents of i-deals is concerning for several important reasons. First, if i-deals can refer to negotiated arrangements about relatively minor terms of the employment relationship, then they are likely too trivial, widespread, and mundanely available to be described as idiosyncratic or valuable. For example, flexibility i-deals (Bal et al., 2012; Hornung et al., 2008) do not seem noteworthy of a major shift in employment terms and may simply reflect institutionally available options such as working part time, which in some countries (e.g., the UK) employees have a legal entitlement to request part-time work. Similarly, task i-deals (e.g., Hornung et al., 2011; Rosen et al., 2013) may reflect the routine managerial activity of dividing work across team members. Such i-deals are therefore readily distributed and unlikely to signal special treatment to employees or instill obligations to reciprocate.

In conclusion, the above set of interconnected concerns about the three defining features of i-deals amount to a considerable lack of clarity. These concerns are important because without a clear definition we cannot make clear theoretical predictions, we cannot consistently operationalize i-deals, and practitioners will not know how to enact i-deals in workplaces and the benefits of doing so (or not).

Theoretical mechanisms linking i-deals to employment relationship outcomes

In this section we argue that there is no novel and unique theoretical mechanism linking i-deals to outcomes. Furthermore, the two general theoretical mechanisms (needs and, in particular, social exchange) linking i-deals to outcomes offer ambiguous predictions. Finally, research has insufficiently considered how i-deals may damage employment relations and unit-level productivity.

What is the theoretical mechanism that links i-deals to outcomes? Researchers hypothesize that i-deals will be associated with employee attitudes, behavior, and performance, but do not specify in any precise way what evaluative feature of i-deals explains outcomes. What is it about i-deals that relates to outcomes?

We can again make a useful contrast here with psychological contract research. In psychological contract research, the main construct linking the psychological contract to outcomes was not psychological contracts per se, but the specific construct of psychological contract breach (i.e., when employees perceive the organization to fail to fulfill promised obligations, Conway & Briner, 2005). For i-deals, the research suggests that having an i-deal leads to outcomes, but we have already noted above that the definition of i-deals encapsulates multiple features. So which feature drives outcomes? The definitions of i-deals make reference to an employee the organization values, successful negotiation of benefits, the receipt of benefits themselves, and fulfilling employee needs. These distinct components could all feasibly affect employee attitudes and behaviors, raising questions about what specifically it is about i-deals that affects outcomes. For example, are the positive attitudes associated with i-deals a result of the actual negotiation process or the benefits resulting from the i-deal?

Researchers commonly refer to the two general mechanisms of social exchange and fulfilling employee needs when making i-deals predictions. Dealing first with needs, while needs are often referred to in the definitions and texts, the references are brief, general, and often taken to be read as self-evident in benefitting parties. There is therefore very little substantial material to get our teeth into here, other than to say that the needs mechanism is underspecified and underproblematized. For instance, if i-deals have benefits through satisfying needs, then which needs precisely, as there are many needs and indeed typologies of needs (Maslow, McClelland, etc.). It is also worth noting that the theoretical value of needs and need theories have well-documented limitations, such as vaguely defined concepts, being impossible to refute, and appearing to explain all behavior, yet offering no clear basis for predicting any behavior (see, for example, Salancik & Pfeffer, 1977; Wahba & Bridwell, 1976).

Turning to social exchange as a general mechanism, it is commonly deployed when explaining the effects of i-deals on employee attitudes and behavior. Is its application to i-deals compelling? The argument in part rests on whether i-deals are beneficial in creating obligations in the recipient to reciprocate (Anand et al., 2010; Liu et al., 2013; Ng & Feldman, 2012b). However, as previously mentioned, it is unclear whether i-deals are governed by mutual benefit or more driven by organizations' attempting to satisfy the needs of employees. As Liu et al. (2013, p. 833) note "the willingness of employers to cater to individual employees needs signals to employees that they are special and worthy of employers' special treatment." This resembles what has been referred to as a communal relationship (Clark & Mills, 1979), in which the giving of benefits is driven by the desire to meet the needs of the other party and without the expectation that these benefits will be reciprocated. If so, then the assumption that i-deals instill obligations in recipients to reciprocate may well be erroneous. Furthermore, if i-deals are viewed by employees as a reward for past contributions, then the recipient may feel entitled to any additional benefits received with little felt obligation to reciprocate.

Finally, we note that the potentially damaging effects of i-deals at the individual and unit level have been insufficiently considered. At the individual level, the positive correlation identified in some empirical studies between i-deals and employee attitudes and behaviors has been interpreted by researchers as reflecting how the recipients of i-deals report more positive attitudes and behaviors; however, an equally plausible alternative interpretation is that the positive correlation found reflects the majority of employees who do not receive i-deals in the work unit reporting lowered morale as a result of making unfavorable social comparisons to recipients of i-deals. Employees consciously and unconsciously make social comparisons to others they work closely with and these processes profoundly shape employee attitudes and behavior (Adams, 1965; Festinger, 1954; Goodman, 1977; Salancik & Pfeffer, 1978). I-deals researchers draw on processes of favorable social comparisons to explain why the small number of recipients of i-deals report more positive attitudes and behaviors (e.g., Ng & Feldman, 2010, 2012a, 2012b, 2013); by the same token, the majority of employees will not receive i-deals and will presumably be making unfavorable and likely demoralizing social comparisons, resulting in less positive attitudes and behaviors. There are many compelling theoretical reasons for suspecting that offering i-deals to a select few may negatively affect the majority of employees who *do not* receive the i-deal, such as believing an injustice has taken place and/or the psychological contract has been violated. This in turn would damage their motivation and behaviors towards the organization and their peers, perhaps especially helping behaviors towards those employees who indeed receive i-deals.

There is some evidence to support this view. Broschak and Davis-Blake's (2006) study of two large, multinational financial organizations in the United States found that the degree of heterogeneity of employment arrangements in a work group (mixing standard and nonstandard workers in the same work group) had significant negative effects on employee-to-supervisor relations, coworker relations, and helping behaviors and a positive effect on the intention to leave. The authors concluded that "nonstandard work arrangements designed to retain valued employees may negatively affect work group relations ... creating an idiosyncratic deal in order to keep an individual involved in an ongoing work group may in fact cause intragroup relations to deteriorate" (Broschack & Davis-Blake, 2006, p. 389). This suggests that while some lucky workers benefit from their individual i-deals, individuals in the wider group or unit may experience losses, which could lead to a negative overall effect for the unit's productivity. The unit as an aggregate is perhaps particularly likely to suffer, as coworker relations and helping behaviors take a hit and the social and psychological climate suffers.

It is odd that justice perceptions have not yet been empirically examined alongside i-deals. The awareness that an employee has obtained an i-deal is likely to raise justice concerns amongst his/her colleagues as we note above and has been noted elsewhere (Greenberg et al., 2004). We considered distributive justice, however, other researchers note concerns relating to other justice dimensions. For example, Greenberg, Roberge, Ho, and Rousseau (2004) argue that to mitigate the potential negative effects, all employees should be treated consistently so that they all have the opportunity to negotiate an i-deal. If making the opportunity for all employees to negotiate i-deals facilitates procedural justice, what is the implication of this for the nature of the deal itself? Rather than being a coveted deal reserved for highly valued employees, it becomes a widespread minor deal on offer to all.

Injustice is but one possible downside to i-deals. To date, the outcomes focus on the positive consequences of i-deals with little consideration of a fuller range of negative outcomes. For example, an employee sensing that a few coworkers are receiving i-deals without knowing the specific terms may feel paranoid, jealous, and envious. For the i-deal recipient, it may encourage individualism, self-interest, and a heightened sense of entitlement. Research that considers coworkers' views of those receiving i-deals suggests that i-deals thrive in (and generate?) environments of self-interest. Lai et al. (2009) found that coworkers were more likely to accept their colleague receiving an i-deal when the colleague is a close friend and when they believe it increases their chance of a comparable future opportunity. The effects of i-deals on organizational outcomes were found to be stronger for people high on individualism (Liu et al., 2013).

In summary, there is a need for better theorizing on the multilevel effects of i-deals, notably the individual-level effects and the group-level effects. I-deals may be associated with benefits for those who receive them, but bring significant losses for those who do not, which, given they constitute the majority of a work group, may lower the overall unit's performance. Hence coworkers (i.e., the majority of employees not receiving i-deals in the unit), the unit in aggregate, and the organization may lose out.

Concerns about the designs and measures used to empirically research i-deals

Here we first identify concerns about survey measures used to research i-deals and second raise concerns about the broader research designs employed.

Regarding the survey measures, our first observation is that i-deals have not been consistently measured – there is little agreement about how to measure i-deals and little interest in full measurement validation studies (see Rosen et al., 2013, for an exception). Considerable variation exists as reflected in the following: some measures require respondents to comment on exchange items that are "different from his/her coworkers" (Anand et al., 2010), some require respondents to rate the extent to which they had "asked for and successfully negotiated individual arrangements different from their peers" (Hornung et al., 2008), and others require respondents to rate the extent the organization has "promised a level of [the item, e.g., pay] that most employees in my team/unit do not get" (Ng & Feldman, 2012).

Second, and related to the previous point, none of the measures are true to its definition, which requires i-deals to be individually negotiated, different from peers, and mutually beneficial. I-deals measures variously capture one of these features, but not two or more. The measures have therefore not operationalized crucial defining features of the definition of i-deals.

Third, the range of content of i-deals terms/dimensions varies considerably across studies. In some studies the range of content is very narrow, capturing one or two terms (typically flexibility, development), whereas in other studies up to six terms are captured (e.g., pay, advancement opportunities, skill training, career development opportunities, a level of job security, support for personal problems; Ng & Feldman, 2010, 2012a). I-deals are defined as very wide ranging, so why such narrow operationalizations? The measures need to better capture the wide breadth of content of i-deals.

Fourth, the items do not indicate a clear time frame over which the respondent is expected to consider the striking of the i-deal. We do not know therefore whether the respondent is recalling an i-deal negotiation from relatively recently or several years ago. Clearly, the timing of the negotiation is important as to how accurately the event will be recalled and its relevance in predicting employee attitudes and behaviors.

Finally, the incidence/reported levels of i-deals are frequently at improbably high levels given that i-deals are supposed to be "special" and idiosyncratic (e.g., 3.30 on a 7-point Likert type scale,[2] strongly disagree (1) to strongly agree (7), Anand et al., 2010; ranging from 3.83 to 3.90 across 6 measures on a 5-point scale, strongly disagree (1) to strongly agree (5), Ng & Feldman, 2012b). The high levels of reported i-deals do not credibly reflect the idea that they are received by a chosen few, which would dictate a low base rate phenomenon. Are these measures of i-deals therefore really capturing i-deals as a select negotiation or something much more mundanely available, such as stable perceptions of job characteristics?

These issues are important because they suggest that the studies are measuring different constructs, capturing very different elements of the deal, and fundamentally are not fully consistent with i-deals definitions and therefore not valid proxies for i-deals.

We now turn to research designs used to investigate i-deals. Our first concern here is that i-deals studies have typically neglected to collect multi-source data (e.g., information from both employers and employees simultaneously) and therefore cannot assess whether both parties benefit from an i-deal. To assess i-deals and the impact of i-deals, we require research designs that capture employees' and employers' perceptions of the i-deal, along with both parties' assessments of the benefits.

Data should also be collected from third-party coworkers who make up the wider social group and to explore unit-level effects in addition to individual-level effects. As we noted above, to assess the benefits of i-deals to the organization, we need to know how i-deals affect the wider social group within which the person receiving the i-deal belongs. For example, to what extent do i-deals impact such outcomes as unit/group cohesion, collaboration, psychological climate, and productivity? While a small number of employees receiving an i-deal may report benefits, the larger number of employees not receiving an i-deal may report comparatively more negative attitudes as a result of negative social comparisons made with those who receive i-deals, which may tip the unit into experiencing aggregate losses. It is therefore crucial to simultaneously examine the individual effects of i-deals alongside the unit effects. We need to conduct multilevel studies to see whether units showing high variation in i-deals also have higher unit (indicating positive effects of i-deals) or lower unit (consistent with i-deals associating with felt violation of employees not receiving i-deals) performance and other outcomes.

Our second concern is that i-deal measures confound several components, of which we consider two here: the negotiation accompanying the i-deal and the actual reward received resulting from the negotiation. It is therefore unclear which of these two components are causing the effects associated with i-deals measures: Are the effects of i-deals found in studies the result of negotiating the i-deal or a result of what the employee actually gets? For example, if an employee negotiates pay in excess of their peers, the fact that the employee has successfully negotiated an i-deal may lead to feelings of satisfaction, and the increase in pay resulting from the i-deal may also lead to feelings of satisfaction. Therefore, research needs to isolate the effects of the negotiation of the deal per se from what is received. Research designs need to measure the negotiation component and the rewards components when examining i-deals in order to capture the unique effects of each on outcomes.

I-deals research designs need to consider reverse causality issues. Research assumes that i-deals lead to positive outcomes such as employee motivation, commitment, and performance; however, these attitudes and behaviors are also the reasons why employees are offered i-deals and are therefore just as likely to be the causes of i-deals. We need to consider these possibilities and the longer-term trajectories of employee attitudes and behavior. If the award of an i-deal does little to significantly alter the trajectory of employee attitudes and behavior over time, then the i-deal is having no effect; however, in such cases cross-sectional or limited time-point longitudinal data will likely record spurious associations between i-deals and "outcomes."

Last but not least, i-deals research is characterized by cross-sectional, self-report, single-source designs. The limitations of such designs are well-documented (e.g., see Conway & Briner [2005] for how such designs are limited for examining social exchange ideas) and are a general concern in management research, so we will not go into any depth here. In brief, such designs are inappropriate for validly measuring many types of phenomena (such as exchange) examining events, processes, and causality.

Conclusions

We have presented a wide range of critical observations. In essence, i-deals are unclearly defined, so we do not know what i-deals are. There are major inconsistencies across i-deal measures and none of the measures capture all its features, and we are unsure as to whether and how i-deals affect parties to the negotiation and third parties. Indeed, there are good reasons for suspecting i-deals to be detrimental to coworkers and organizations, and existing findings used to support the positive effects of i-deals may in fact indicate that i-deals drive down the attitudes of non-recipients via unfavorable social comparisons.

In a similar manner to the way researchers criticized advocates of models of the flexible firm and flexible employment contracts for moving confusingly between description, prediction, and prescription (see Pollert, 1988), statements about i-deals flit between describing them as a growing trend in organizations, as a way to explain how to motivate contributions in recipients, and as a prescription to organizations about how to retain valued workers. In any case, at present we think i-deals fall short on all fronts. I-deals are too loosely defined to precisely describe activity, there is no clear theory to link i-deals with employee contributions, and the commonly used social exchange theory suggests – at best – mixed effects on outcomes. Given the failure to describe and predict, we're not in a position to prescribe i-deals to organizations.

Notes

1 Neil Conway, School of Management, Royal Holloway University of London, United Kingdom; Jacqueline Coyle-Shapiro, London School of Economics, United Kingdom.
2 As an aside, the use of Likert scales is perhaps inappropriate as i-deals are more likely to be experienced as discrete events and should be measured as such, rather than as strength of agreement.

References

Adams, J.S. (1965). Inequity in social exchange. *Advances in Experimental Social Psychology, 2*, 267–299.

Anand, S., Vidyarthi, P.R., Liden, R.C., & Rousseau, D.M. (2010). Good citizens in poor-quality relationships: Idiosyncratic deals as a substitute for relationship quality. *Academy of Management Journal, 53(5)*, 970–988.

Bal, P.M., De Jong, S.B., Jansen, P.G.W., & Bakker, A.B. (2012). Motivating employees to work beyond retirement: A multi-level study of the role of i-deals and unit climate. *Journal of Management Studies, 49*, 306–331. doi:10.1111/j.1467–6486.2011.01026.x

Bidwell, M., Briscoe, F., Fernandez-Mateo, I., & Sterling, A. (2013). The employment relationship and inequality: How and why changes in employment practices are reshaping rewards in organizations. *Academy of Management Annals, 7(1)*, 61–121.

Broschak, J.P., & Davis-Blake, A. (2006). Mixing standard work and nonstandard deals: The consequences of heterogeneity in employment arrangements. *Academy of Management Journal, 49(2)*, 371–393.

Clark, M.S., & Mills, J. (1979). Interpersonal attraction in exchange and communal relationships. *Journal of Personality and Social Psychology, 37(1)*, 12–24.

Conway, N., & Briner, R.B. (2005). *Understanding psychological contracts at work: A critical evaluation of theory and research*. Oxford: Oxford University Press.

Festinger, L. (1954). A theory of social comparison processes. *Human Relations, 7*, 114–140.

Goodman, P.S. (1977). Social comparison processes in organizations. In B. M. Staw & G. R. Salancik (Eds.), *New directions in organizational behavior* (pp. 97–132). Chicago, IL: St. Clair Press.

Greenberg, J., Roberge, M., Ho, V.T., & Rousseau, D.M. (2004). Fairness in idiosyncratic work arrangements: Justice as an i-deal. In J.J. Martocchio (Ed.), *Research in personnel and human resources management* (Vol. 23, pp. 1–34). Amsterdam: Elsevier.

Hornung, S., Glaser, J., Rousseau, D.M., Angerer, P., & Weigl, M. (2011). Employee-oriented leadership and quality of working life: Mediating roles of idiosyncratic deals. *Psychological Reports, 108(1)*, 59–74.

Hornung, S., Rousseau, D.M., & Glaser, J. (2008). Creating flexible work arrangements through idiosyncratic deals. *Journal of Applied Psychology, 93*, 655–664.

Hornung, S., Rousseau, D.M., & Glaser, J. (2009). Why supervisors make idiosyncratic deals: Antecedents and outcomes of i-deals from a managerial perspective. *Journal of Managerial Psychology, 24*(8), 738–764.

Hornung, S., Rousseau, D.M., Glaser, J., Angerer, P., & Weigl, M. (2010). Beyond top-down and bottom-up work redesign: Customizing job content through idiosyncratic deals. *Journal of Organizational Behavior, 31*(2-3), 187–215.

Lai, L., Rousseau, D.M., & Chang, K.T.T. (2009). Idiosyncratic deals: Coworkers as interested third parties. *Journal of Applied Psychology, 94*(2), 547–556.

Lawler, E.E., & Finegold, D. (2000). Individualizing the organization: Past, present, and future. *Organizational Dynamics, 29*, 1–15.

Lee, C., & Hui, C. (2011). Antecedents and consequences of idiosyncratic deals: A frame of resource exchange. *Frontiers of Business Research in China, 5*(3), 380–401.

Liao, C., Wayne, S.J., & Rousseau, D.M. (2014). Idiosyncratic deals in contemporary organizations: A qualitative and meta-analytical review. *Journal of Organizational Behavior, in press*.

Liu, J., Lee, C., Hui, C., Kwan, H.K., & Wu, L.-Z. (2013). Idiosyncratic deals and employee outcomes: The mediating roles of social exchange and self-enhancement and the moderating role of individualism. *Journal of Applied Psychology, 98*(5), 832–840.

Miner, A.S. (1987). Idiosyncratic jobs in formalized organizations. *Administrative Science Quarterly, 32*, 327–351.

Ng, T.W.H., & Feldman, D.C. (2010). Idiosyncratic deals and organizational commitment. *Journal of Vocational Behavior, 76*, 419–427.

Ng, T.W.H., & Feldman, D.C. (2012a). Breaches of past promises, current job alternatives, and promises of future idiosyncratic deals: Three-way interaction effects on organizational commitment. *Human Relations, 65*(11), 1463–1486.

Ng, T.W.H., & Feldman, D.C. (2012b). Idiosyncratic deals and voice behaviour. *Journal of Management*. doi:10.1177/0149206312457824

Pink, D. (2002). *Free-agent nation: The future of working for yourself*. New York: Warner.

Pollert, A. (1988). The flexible firm: Fixation or fact? *Work, Employment & Society, 2*(3), 281–316.

Rosen, C.C., Slater, D.J., Chang, C.-H., & Johnson, R.E. (2013). Let's make a deal: Development and validation of the ex post i-deals scale. *Journal of Management, 39*(3), 709–742.

Rosen, S. (1981). The economics of superstars. *American Economic Review, 71*, 845–858.

Rousseau, D.M. (1989). Psychological and implied contracts in organizations. *Employee Responsibilities and Rights Journal, 2*(2), 121–139.

Rousseau, D.M. (2001). The idiosyncratic deal: Flexibility versus fairness? *Organizational Dynamics, 29*(4), 260–273.

Rousseau, D.M. (2004). Under the table deals: Preferential, unauthorized or idiosyncratic? In A. O'Leary-Kelly & R. Griffin (Eds.), *The dark side of organizational behavior* (pp. 262–290). San Francisco, CA: Jossey-Bass.

Rousseau, D.M. (2005). *I-deals: Idiosyncratic deals employees bargain for themselves*. New York: M.E. Sharpe.

Rousseau, D.M., Ho, V.T., & Greenberg, J. (2006). I-deals: Idiosyncratic terms in employment relationships. *Academy of Management Review, 31*, 977–994.

Rousseau, D.M., Hornung, S., & Kim, T.G. (2009). Idiosyncratic deals: Testing propositions on timing, content, and the employment relationship. *Journal of Vocational Behavior, 74*, 338–348.

Rousseau, D.M., & Kim, T.G. (2006). *When workers bargain for themselves: Idiosyncratic deals and the nature of the employment relationship*. Paper presented at the British Academy of Management, Belfast.

Salancik, G.R., & Pfeffer, J. (1977). An examination of need-satisfaction models of job attitudes. *Administrative Science Quarterly, 22*, 427–456.

Salancik, G.R., & Pfeffer, J. (1978). A social information processing approach to job attitudes and task design. *Administrative Science Quarterly, 22*, 224–253.

Vidyarthi, P.R., Chaudhry, A., Anand, S., & Liden, R.C. (2014). Flexibility i-deals: how much is ideal? *Journal of Managerial Psychology, 29*(3), 246–265.

Wahba, M.A., & Bridwell, L.G. (1976). Maslow reconsidered: A review of research on the need hierarchy theory. *Organizational Behavior and Human Performance, 15*(2), 212–240.

5

AN I-DEAL CAREER

On the relationship between i-deals and career development

Aukje Nauta and Cristel van de Ven[1]

Introduction

Mark[2] is an educational manager from a Dutch company who has successfully set up an internal company academy to train and educate the employees of this company. The academy is nowadays running smoothly, and therefore Mark is searching for new challenges in his work and for career development opportunities. He could apply for a new job outside his company, but, for several reasons, this is currently not attractive to him. He wants to see the company academy running smoothly in the next few years; moreover, he feels highly committed to his own company. Therefore, he thinks of something different: he wants to propose to his supervisor to contract him to other companies for one or two days a week to help these companies set up their own academy. To him, this sounds like an offer his company cannot refuse. His company will save money and profit from what Mark will learn from other companies, which will likely increase the quality of Mark's work in his own company. And for Mark, this developmental arrangement will give him the opportunity to broaden his skillset and to enhance his professional network. Mark believes that this will help him to make future career steps.

The example above illustrates a potential idiosyncratic deal or i-deal: an individual agreement about work content, personal development, or working conditions that employees negotiate with their supervisor (Rousseau, 2005). An i-deal deviates from standard work rules and regulations and from agreements made by one's colleagues, which explains the term "idiosyncratic." None of Mark's colleagues is currently contracted to another company; it is an individual wish of Mark's, which fits to his current career aspirations. He is ready for a new challenge that he can combine with his current job. If Mark will actually close this deal with his supervisor, it can only be labeled an i-deal if it meets the interests of both Mark and the company. In advance, Mark assumes that this will be the case. Surely, the deal will be good for his own career development; the company will profit from what Mark will learn in other companies and will also save money due to the fact that Mark will earn money for the company with his secondment. Mark also assumes that his direct colleagues will not be disadvantaged, because Mark is currently capable of doing his job within three to four days a week. Hence, nobody will have a greater workload if Mark should be contracted elsewhere for one or two days a week. A question is: will his supervisor see the advantages of this deal as well? Hence, prior to closing an i-deal, parties will have to talk and negotiate with each other. An employee and his or her supervisor have to mutually explore the wishes, interests, and opportunities with regard to work, career development, and working conditions, until they close a deal that meets the three-fold interests of the employee, the organization, and the coworkers (Rousseau, 2005).

I-deals and organizational justice

A core dilemma within employment relations in general and i-deals especially is concerned with organizational justice (Greenberg, Roberge, Ho, & Rousseau, 2004). If employees feel unjustly treated, decreased work satisfaction and performance are often the result. Justice often implies equal treatment. The concept of "equal pay for equal work," a slogan often used by trade unions, refers to this justice principle. But employees differ strongly from each other; they have different needs with regard especially to the content of their job, working hours, and personal and career development. To illustrate the latter: some employees prefer to follow formal training and education; others prefer to learn informally, via challenging projects, coaching, or peer consultation. And some people prefer horizontal career steps, whereas others focus on vertical career ladders. Hence, the justice principle of equality does not sufficiently take individual differences into account. In the above example of Mark, the justice principle of "need" is more applicable. Mark apparently feels the need to be contracted, otherwise he wouldn't suggest it, whereas his colleagues seem to feel this need less strongly since they don't mention the idea of a secondment in conversations with their supervisor. In other cases, such as decisions on who to promote, the justice principle of "competence" (who has the best skills and competences for the job) seems more right. These three justice principles – equality, need, and competence – sometimes clash. For example, suppose that Mark's supervisor refuses his idea of a secondment, stating that "No other employee in this company has ever been contracted to other organizations before," an argument that refers to the justice principle of equality. Mark would likely be disappointed, because as an individual with specific needs, he does not feel recognized and valued. Rousseau (2001) describes this dilemma of consistency and equal treatment on the one hand versus the need for flexibility on the other hand as a problem that cannot be solved. Rather, this dilemma is a fact to be managed by the parties involved. This implies that fair employment relations are a matter of constant negotiation, dialogue, and conflict management.

Trends on the labor market that increase the relevance of i-deals

Although research on i-deals and career development is scarce, we propose that i-deals will become more and more important for career development in the near future, for two reasons. The first reason refers to current rapid technological developments. Diamandis and Kotler (2012) describe how technology often develops along exponential curves. At first, technological developments appear to go slowly, but from a certain point on, they accelerate. Specific technologies improve and spread with high speed, allowing applications to become cheaper and cheaper. Think of the introduction of broadband Internet some decades ago. Another example is 3D printing. This was unthinkable a few years ago. But recently, plastic parts for a skull transplant have been successfully printed and transplanted in a patient who was suffering from extra bone growth inside her skull (www.umcutrecht.nl, 27 March 2014). It is expected that within a few years, many people will have a 3D printer at home, for example to print furniture parts, glasses, Lego blocks, etc. Due to exponential technological developments like these, job content and work processes change constantly. It is to be expected that the "half-life" of jobs becomes shorter and shorter. Even such "old" jobs as teacher might change radically, when "massive open online courses" (MOOCs) become the norm in schools and universities. For example, maybe only excellent teachers will be employed for video courses, whereas other teachers become one-on-one mentors and still others will constantly develop new ways of learning. In sum, exponential technological growth causes work to change faster and faster, which requires constant adaptability from employees. Successful career development depends more and more on flexibility, creativity, and knowledge: competences that people can develop best if they themselves can (co)determine the type and content of their job and their preferred ways of working and learning, for example by making i-deals about it.

A second reason why i-deals are likely to be important for career development is associated with the increase of the retirement age. Across Europe, many employees used to retire around the age of 60 or even earlier. However, due to an aging population in Europe, early retirement arrangements have been abolished, because they became too expensive. As a result, the perspective of workers is currently changing. Many employees around the age of 55 used to ask each other questions like: "How long do you still have to work?" Now that most employees have to work until the age of 65 or, in some European countries, even until the age of 67, older workers start asking each other different questions, such as: "What are your career plans for the future?" De Lange and colleagues (2011), following Lang and Carstensen (2002), refer to this phenomenon as a constraint versus an open-ended time perspective. People with an open-ended time perspective (also called a "time since birth" perspective) are more strongly motivated to develop themselves and to search for new experiences than people with a constrained time perspective (a "time till death" perspective). Instead, the latter focuses more on short-term emotion-related goals, such as deepening one's current relationships (De Lange, Bal, Van der Heijden,

De Jong, & Schaufeli, 2011). Now that the formal retirement age is increasing and will continue to increase in the future, there is neither an early, nor a clear, limit to paid work. Without such a limit, people are more likely to keep an open-ended time perspective with regard to work. Whether they like it or not, people have to keep on developing themselves until high ages. However, older people have already chosen certain career paths, and some of them experience a deterioration of (physical) abilities. Hence, the older people are, the less they fit in standardized jobs. To be able to work until high age, many employees therefore have to search for creative solutions (i.e., i-deals) to compensate for decreasing abilities and/or to stay intrinsically motivated to work. Research by Bal, De Jong, Jansen, and Bakker (2012) shows that if older workers make i-deals about flexibility and development, they will be more highly motivated to work even after the formal retirement age. Hence, i-deals can stimulate workers to continue to develop their career, even at ages at which people used to think about retiring.

I-deals and career development

When exploring the relationships between i-deals and career development, we distinguish between two main types of i-deals: challenge versus comfort. The first type of i-deals challenges people to develop their knowledge and skills and are therefore likely to contribute to career development. For example, an employee of a Dutch municipality once got the chance to lead a special project in which she had to coordinate dialogue sessions with various organizations and institutions on the difficult issue of cutting municipal budgets. This project was quite a challenge for the employee, because it was totally different from her regular job. The project demanded much of her political and social skills; skills she had hardly used before doing her regular tasks. Other examples of challenge i-deals are special training opportunities and internships within one's own or another organization, as to explore opportunities for a career transition. Challenge i-deals combine earlier identified categories of i-deals (Hornung et al., 2010), such as developmental i-deals (e.g., following an extraordinary course) and task i-deals (e.g., doing a special project).

The second type of i-deals, comfort i-deals, is intended to make work less demanding or to bridge career and private life. These type of i-deals are focused on solving a specific problem, for example, when an employee has health problems (Ng & Feldman, 2010; Rosen, Slater, Chang, & Johnson, 2013) or experiences a work–life misbalance. Examples of comfort i-deals are reduced work load, increased support from colleagues or one's supervisor, and special arrangements to balance work and family interests, for example working from home or on special hours. Comfort i-deals are expected to add nothing to or even harm career development, since they do not stimulate the development of new knowledge and skills. Also, comfort i-deals could function as "golden chains": personalized terms of employment that "fit like a glove" and therefore will prevent employees from making career steps, since they might not be willing to give up this unique deal when making a career transition. For example, someone who is allowed to work from home during school hours, or who performs easier tasks against his or her usual pay, will experience little incentive to make a vertical or even horizontal career step. Such a career step would likely imply increased commuting time or decreased pay. Comfort i-deals combine earlier identified categories of i-deals, such as flexibility i-deals, e.g., working from home (Hornung, Rousseau, & Glaser, 2008; Hornung et al., 2010), and financial i-deals, e.g. receiving special bonuses or benefits (Rousseau, Ho, & Greenberg, 2006).

How important are challenge i-deals for career development? First results of studies on the consequences of i-deals show that challenging i-deals – e.g., developmental i-deals – lead employees to show more so-called organizational citizenship behavior (OCB; Anand, Vidyarthi, Liden, & Rousseau, 2010). OCB is behavior that serves one's colleagues and the organization, but extends a formal job description (Organ, Podsakoff, & MacKenzie, 2006). Podsakoff, Whiting, Podsakoff, and Blume (2009) showed that OCB leads to higher supervisor judgments and pay, two aspects that contribute to career prospects. Hence, we can infer from this research that challenge i-deals might contribute to career development.

In a recent study that we performed among 99 dyads of employees and supervisors working in university medical centers or banks, we found that challenging deals (e.g., extra training, mentoring, and/or challenging tasks) increase supervisors' assessment of employees' promotability, six months after having negotiated these deals during job conversations, over and above supervisors' assessment of employees' promotability just before the job conversation. Comfort i-deals, i.e., deals that spared the employee, were not related to promotability assessments of the supervisor (van de Ven, Van Vianen, Nauta, & De Pater, 2014).

The increasing importance of i-deals for career development is not without risks. It could lead to a "law of the strongest." Hornung (2011) warned for a so-called "Matthew-effect" that is associated with i-deals, namely the danger of a cumulative (dis)advantage for certain groups of employees. This refers to Matthew 13:12 in the Bible: *Whoever has will be given more, and he will have in abundance. Whoever does not have, even what he has will be taken from him.* Applied to i-deals, this metaphor means that the law of the strongest i-dealer will apply. Strong negotiators know how to successfully negotiate a challenge i-deal, which increases their career chances, which will make it even easier to get more i-deals in the future. In contrast, people who cannot negotiate very well will not get i-deals, with lower career chances as a result. Therefore, it is important that HR managers steer i-deal–making practices in the right direction.

Managing i-deals

How can HR managers steer i-deal–making processes in the right direction, especially in relation to career development? Ideally, HR managers choose a mediating role. The core of i-deal making is a creative dialogue between an employee and his or her superior. In an open, transparent, and creative dialogue, there is a high probability of a fair i-deal–making process, from which employee, organization, and coworkers may profit. An HR manager can facilitate such an open, creative dialogue in several ways. For example, an HR manager who knows about low job satisfaction in a specific department, after having studied the results of an employee survey, can visit this department. She can apply an intervention in which employees and managers learn to talk about possible improvements at work and with regard to team and personal development. Another possibility is that HR managers support individual employees in preparing an i-deal, using role plays to practice negotiations with their supervisors. Maybe the aforementioned Mark could use such support, because it is likely that his supervisor will not immediately embrace Mark's very unusual proposal. For example, Mark's supervisor may have doubts about Mark's loyalty or about the probability that Mark will be hired by other companies for the task of setting up an internal academy. During a role play, Mark could learn to deal with different arguments that his supervisor will come up with. In a mediating role, HR managers who are trusted by both the employee and his or her supervisor can act as facilitators in mutual i-deal conversations (See Box 1). This implies that the HR manager functions as a party that is not (only) serving as an organizational agent, but as a neutral party that serves the interests of both manager and employee. If employees do not see HR as a neutral party, the facilitating role can be outsourced to professional, external mediators. In that situation, HR can play an important role in selecting the right external mediators for this task.

Box 1. Dialogue coaching

Dialogue coaching implies that internal or external experts act as facilitators during formal conversations, such as appraisal interviews or career conversations, between employees and supervisors. The role of the expert is to observe, to intervene as soon as a conversation is not running smoothly, and to give feedback afterwards. The expert uses conflict mediation techniques to improve the dialogue. For example, if the expert perceives that one party is constantly interrupting the other party, the expert can intervene by asking the other party how he experiences these interruptions. Or the expert might notice that none of the parties is writing down any of the agreements (i-deals) they make. The expert might then ask whether it would be a good idea to take notes, to make sure that everybody knows the agreements (i-deals) made, and how to follow them up. A second way of dialogue coaching is to videotape conversations and discuss the video afterwards, together with the employee and the supervisor. The expert may select fragments in which the conversation is running smoothly. Our own experience as dialogue coaches is that even when parties watch positive fragments of themselves, they see room for improvement. Most of the time, watching three to four fragments is sufficient. A supervisor who watches his own behavior on videotape might say "I see myself nodding all the time," after which the employee might say: "That gives me the impression that you are really listening to me." Dialogue coaching is part of our research project, in which we will analyze relationships between dialogue, i-deals, and employability, with the help of videotapes and short questionnaires applied to employees and supervisors during and after mutual conversations.

Conclusion

In this chapter, we argued, based on scarce research, that i-deals can be important for career development, especially now that employees have to work until a high age, in jobs that are asking more and more for knowledge and creativity. Such i-deals should be more about challenging and less about making work less demanding for the employee. If sparing the employee is nevertheless needed, for example due to personal or physical problems, it is important to combine a so-called "comfort i-deal" with a "challenge i-deal." "It is fine with me that you quit the hard work next year, but what else can we agree upon, to ensure that this temporary alleviation will not hurt your performance and promotability in the long run?" A question like this should belong to the repertoire of all supervisors. This and other open questions are part of an open, transparent, and creative dialogue between employees and supervisors. Such an open dialogue is not self-evident. HR managers can facilitate dialogues like this. If they succeed in playing a mediating role during i-deal–making processes, then everybody – from high to low, from specialist to generalist – will be able to make a challenging i-deal.

Epilogue

What happened to Mark, who wanted to close an i-deal? Did he succeed in making an i-deal with his supervisor? Yes, although the final deal looked different from what Mark had expected in advance. Mark's company had to downsize. The internal academy then gained importance, not only to educate employees, but also to guide some of them in transitions from their old job to a new job outside the company. In the beginning, Mark was very busy with this project. But as soon as all outplacements were completed, Mark got the opportunity to acquire a secondment assignment for himself. This turned out to be very successful; his secondment portfolio increased rapidly. Mark was able to slowly reduce his job from five days a week, to four, to three, to two days a week. As soon as his employer had to downsize further and outplace Mark as well, Mark was able to run his own consultancy. Thanks to the i-deals he made – a challenge i-deal on being contracted to other companies, combined with a comfort i-deal on reducing work hours – Mark's career flourishes.

Notes

1 Aukje Nauta, University of Amsterdam, the Netherlands; Cristel van de Ven, Factor Vijf, the Netherlands.
2 The story of Mark is partly based on reality; Mark is not his real name.

References

Anand, S., Vidyarthi, P.R., Liden, R.C., & Rousseau, D.M. (2010). Good citizens in poor-quality relationships: Idiosyncratic deals as a substitute for relationship quality. *Academy of Management Journal, 53*, 970–988.

Bal, P.M., De Jong, S.B., Jansen, P.G.W., & Bakker, A.B. (2012). Motivating employees to work beyond retirement: A multi-level study of the role of i-deals and unit climate. *Journal of Management Studies, 49*, 306–331.

De Lange, A.H., Bal, P.M., Van der Heijden, B.I.J.M., De Jong, N., & Schaufeli, W.B. (2011). When I'm 64: Psychological contract breach, work motivation and the moderating roles of future time perspective and regulatory focus. *Work & Stress, 25*(4), 338–354.

Diamandis, P.H., & Kotler, S. (2012). *Abundance: The future is better than you think*. New York: Free Press.

Greenberg, J., Roberge, M.E., Ho, V.T, & Rousseau, D.M. (2004) Fairness as an i-deal: Justice in under-the-table employment arrangements. *Research in Personnel and Human Resources Management, 22*, 1–34.

Hornung, S. (2011, August 15). *Idiosyncratic deals and employability: A multifaceted relationship*. Presentation at the 71st Academy of Management Meeting, San Antonio, TX.

Hornung, S., Glaser, J., Rousseau, D.M., Angerer, P., & Weigl, M. (2011). Employee-oriented leadership and quality of working life: Mediating roles of idiosyncratic deals. *Psychological Reports, 108*, 59–74.

Hornung, S., Rousseau, D.M., & Glaser, J. (2008). Creating flexible work arrangements through idiosyncratic deals. *Journal of Applied Psychology, 93*, 655–664.

Hornung, S., Rousseau, D.M., Glaser, J., Angerer, P., & Weigl, M. (2010). Beyond top-down and bottom-up work redesign: Customizing job content through idiosyncratic deals. *Journal of Organizational Behavior, 31*(2–3), 187–215.

Lang, F.R., & Carstensen, L.L. (2002). Time counts: Future time perspective, goals and social relationships. *Psychology and Aging, 17*(1), 125–139.

Ng, T.W.H., & Feldman, D.C. (2010). Idiosyncratic deals and organizational commitment. *Journal of Vocational Behavior, 76*, 419–427.

Organ, D.W., Podsakoff, P.M., & MacKenzie, S.B. (2006). *Organizational citizenship behavior: Its nature, antecedents, and consequences*. London: Sage.

Podsakoff, N.P., Whiting, S.W., Podsakoff, Ph. M., & Blume, B.D. (2009). Individual- and organizational-level consequences of organizational citizenship behaviors: A meta-analysis. *Journal of Applied Psychology, 94*, 122–141.

Rosen, C.C., Slater, D.J., Chang, C.-H., & Johnson, R.E. (2013). Let's make a deal: Development and validation of the ex post i-deals scale. *Journal of Management, 39*(3), 709–742.

Rousseau, D.M. (2001). The idiosyncratic deal: Flexibility versus fairness. *Organizational Dynamics, 29*, 260–273.

Rousseau, D.M. (2005). *I-deals: Idiosyncratic deals employees bargain for themselves*. New York: M.E. Sharpe.

Rousseau, D.M., Ho, V.T., & Greenberg, J. (2006). I-deals: Idiosyncratic terms in employment relationships. *Academy of Management Review, 31*(4), 977–994.

van de Ven, C., Van Vianen, A.E.M., Nauta, A., & De Pater, I.E. (2014). *Deals people make. The antecedents of challenging deals and the effects of these deals on promotability*. Working paper.

6
A STRATEGIC HRM PERSPECTIVE ON I-DEALS

Brigitte Kroon, Charissa Freese, and René Schalk[1]

Introduction

Strategic human resource management (SHRM) is based on the presumption that organizations' human resources are of critical importance to the success of the organization. SHRM aims at aligning employee skills and behaviors of employees with the needs and ambitions of the organization (Boxall & Purcell, 2008). Traditionally this top-down view of SHRM led HR professionals to design policies and procedures in line with the organization's strategy and goals. These find their way into the organization through managers who translate the intended practices into daily practice and are received by employees who then react to the perceived practices with favorable attitudes and behaviors (Wright & Nishii, 2007). However, talented employees with negotiation power often negotiate personalized terms and conditions of employment, differing from standardized HR practices (Jackson, Schuler, & Jiang, 2013). Managers, in their urge to respond quickly to changing environments, respond favorably to individual requests. Therefore, in practice, many variations in terms of employment exist. This illustrates that HRM is not only a top-down process of communicating intended HR practices to employees by means of written-down procedures and managers who *impose* HRM on employees, but also a bottom-up process by which people try to find a match between their own needs and the requirements of the organization. I-deals go beyond understanding individual differences between employees in reactions to HRM (Guest, 2002). Instead, they emphasize the increasing focus on the role of employees in *constructing* HRM. I-deals require employees' input to shape their expectations towards HRM. These paradoxical views on HRM concerning standardized uniform HR practices developed as a logical result from the strategic organizational goals and the bottom-up request for customization by employees are addressed in this chapter.

The outline of the chapter is as follows. First, we position i-deals as a strategic choice within strategic HRM. Second, we present an overview of the benefits and costs of introducing i-deals as part of the HR policies in the organization. We consecutively address the benefits and costs of i-deals on the organizational, team, and individual worker levels. Finally, we discuss the conditions for effectively managing i-deals in organizations.

SHRM theory and i-deals

Strategic HRM concerns all philosophies, policies, and practices and processes applied in organizations to align the behavior of people with the strategic goals of the organization to achieve organizational performance. Strategic HRM contributes to the enhancement of unique human and social capital in terms of knowledge, skills, and abilities (KSAs), motivation and effort, and opportunities to perform within organizations that are difficult to copy by competitors, thus creating the potential of competitive advantage (Jiang et al., 2012; Wright, Dunford, & Snell, 2001).

Most literature on SHRM promotes a systems or bundles approach, in which the various elements of HRM (recruitment, selection, induction, training and development, performance management, remuneration, the organization of work, and employee voice) are combined into one coherent bundle before analyzing the contribution of SHRM to organizational performance (Huselid, 1995; Macduffie, 1995). Two key constituents of effective HRM bundles are synergy and alignment. Synergy implies that the result of the bundle as a whole is larger than the sum of the separate elements: this occurs when the elements have "horizontal fit"; the elements of the HRM bundle are designed in such a way that they are complementary to each other (Delery, 1998; Jiang et al., 2012). Alignment is the extent to which the SHRM bundle relates to the strategy and requirements of the organization; this ("vertical fit") matches the HRM strategy with strategic organizational goals (Gerhart, 2007). This second element can lead to differentiation within organizations, since organizations may consist of subunits with different subgoals.

Often, organizations have different HR systems to manage diverse groups of employees. Clinton and Guest (2013) found that different HRM systems were reported by different job levels in organizations. Proponents of the HR architecture suggest that variation in HRM systems between employee groups should be based on the relative value of their human capital to organizational performance (see Lepak & Snell, 1999). Hence, various systems that are aligned with subunits of people can coexist in one organization. Also, subcultures in organizations and differences in leadership styles cause unit-level variation in the implementation of intended HRM systems within organizations. Indeed, there are repeated observations of functional-level differences in employee reports of HR practices, on top of department-level differences (Arthur & Boyles, 2007). Multilevel approaches to HRM hold that HRM is intended to be similar to all employees at least at the level of focal job-groups, but that attitudes and perceptions may lead to differences in how employees react to HRM (e.g., Wright & Nishii, 2007). However, i-deals go beyond differences between individuals regarding the perception of bundles and refer to real and intentional differences in HRM between employees doing similar work (Rousseau, 2005). In addition to including employees to evaluate HRM implementation, more attention is needed to the way employees contribute to HRM by closing i-deals.

I-deals are made to establish work arrangements that match the needs of individual employees. According to person–environment fit theory, employees are most motivated when their jobs suit their needs and capabilities (Ostroff & Schulte, 2007). In case of an imbalance between work and personal needs, employees actively strive to reach their own fit in several domains (Wrzesniewski & Dutton, 2001). In some cases this may lead employees to request for changes in their terms and conditions of employment. Research revealed four categories of job arrangements that employees can occasionally bargain for. These are financial deals (such as extra salary or a bonus), developmental deals (such as special training or education, promotion), flexibility deals (working at home, or deviant working hours) (Rosen, Slater, Chang, & Johnson, 2011), and special needs deals (support for personal problems; Ng & Feldman, 2008). These categories based on individual needs correspond broadly with the core HR policy domains in SHRM (KSAs, motivation, and opportunity to perform) (Jiang et al., 2012), indicating that aligning individual-level fit with the strategic goals of the organization is possible.

Employee contributions and person–environment fit have been proposed as key determinants of HR philosophy and policies (Lengnick-Hall, Lengnick-Hall, Andrade, & Drake, 2009). However, this level of differentiation of HRM systems at the level of individual employees directs attention to implementation issues in SHRM, in particular when strategic fit is becoming more and more complex (Becker & Huselid, 2006). Strategic fit refers to alignment between the overall business strategy and the HR strategy. I-deals have the potential to optimize fit at the lowest level in the organization. To understand its added value to creating competitive advantage through unique social and human capital, we first investigate similar HRM investments in employees on different levels in the employment relationship, such as the organization and differentiated groups with the organization.

Conceptualizing i-deals within the employment relationship

HR strategy increasingly combines standardized and tailor-made employment arrangements as part of the process of managing human capital. Standardized policies captured in personnel handbooks and formal rules and regulations are aligned with personalized, tailor-made arrangements requested by "new employees" in their search for employment that matches optimally with their lives. In this paragraph, we describe how employment relationships include elements of idiosyncrasy on different organizational levels. For the individual employee, the uniqueness of the total employment benefits package is built up from different levels of customization. Labor laws, such as the entitlement to minimum wages, apply to all employees in a

TABLE 6.1 Customization of Deals within the Employment Relationship

Level	Deal	System	HRM strategy	Initiative
Society	Law	Standard for all employees in the country	Employee protection	Politics, law
Industry	Collective Labor Agreements	Standard for all employees in an industry	Industry standards	Unions, Employer associations
Organization	Uniqueness	Standard for all employees in an organization	Best employer, outside orientation (compared to other organizations)	Strategic management, Works council
Team	Differentiation / We-deal	Differentiated workforce within organization	Groups, marketing approach (top down), internal orientation (relative value of different employee groups)	Strategic management, Employee stakeholder groups
Individual	I-deal	Flexible terms and conditions for individual employees	Bottom up, employee initiated, P–E fit	Individual employees, Line managers

country and are the most standardized form of employment relations. Deeper down the levels, the employment relationship becomes more customized and unique. Each level downwards carries some elements of customization. However, most customization can be found at the lowest level – the level of the individual worker. Table 6.1 summarizes how the different employment relations levels relate to customized employment arrangements.

Organization level: uniqueness of employment conditions

Standardized employment benefits are positioned within collective labor agreements that apply to the organization and national labor laws. Standardized resources are available to all permanent employees in the organization and consist of annual leave, health-care benefits, sick leave, and the like. Employers can offer an excellent standard package of employment conditions to all employees that their employees are not likely to get elsewhere. This relates to what has been called the replicability of the psychological contract (see Ng & Feldman, 2008). This can be seen as an organization-level i-deal. By offering competitive employment conditions, employees perceive psychological contract uniqueness, which they return with favorable attitudes towards the employer (Ng & Feldman, 2008). Psychological contract uniqueness refers to the unique employment conditions that can be obtained at this particular organization as compared to other organizations. The banking industry, for instance, is known for its good employment benefits, including reduced interest rates for mortgages. This sector has unique employment conditions as compared to other sectors. Likewise, organizations such as General Electric are well-known for their management development programs; these are not available in many other companies.

Team or department level: strategic differentiation and we-deals

Position-based resources are only available to certain groups of employees, as a function of their job classification, organizational role, or occupation, and include the distribution of power and access to resources such as management training. This HR differentiation refers to allocating resources differently between groups of employees or between individual employees. Differentiation allows to subject employees to different strategies, goals, or performance indicators to be managed efficiently and effectively (Huselid, 1995; Lepak & Snell, 1999). Diversity programs can also be perceived as a deal that aims to progress socially disadvantaged groups through the hierarchical layers of organizations (Bidwell, Briscoe, Fernandez-Mateo, & Sterling, 2013). Idiosyncratic practices involve, for example, parental leave, which clearly serves to address the needs of particular groups of employees (e.g., parents) to be able to combine work and other responsibilities. Position-based differentiation is a top-down approach of what the organization thinks these groups of employees need in order to perform well in the organization. Most differentiation strategies are developed in the top of organizations. However, bottom-up initiatives of groups of employees can also result in special deals with subunits in the organization. This scenario is referred to as "we"-deals: groups of individual workers join forces to bargain for new favorable conditions of employment as a group, for example, by negotiating for more autonomy in job descriptions (Hornung, Rousseau, & Glaser, 2009).

Individual level: i-deals

Idiosyncratic resources (i-deals) are negotiated employment arrangements at the level of individual employees. They serve to repair imperfect fit between the "standard" terms and conditions of employment and individual needs, such that both the employee and the organizational requirements are satisfied. I-deals may meet certain wishes by individual workers who, for instance, are in a traineeship program to become the future leaders of the organization and might want to work part time to meet family obligations, which is typically not included in these traineeship programs. As compared to organization- or team-based deals, i-deals can contribute best to make the fit between employee needs and the organization (referred to as person–environment fit, Ostroff & Schulte, 2007). As i-deals include an element of negotiation between individual employees and their employer, it is likely that the amount of customization is partly a function of the employee's value to the organization. This directs the attention to questions about the strategic use of customization at the lowest level in the organization.

I-deals in the employment relationship: customization or HR failure?

The largest difference between idiosyncrasy at the individual level versus team – or organizational – level concerns the room for individual negotiation. However, this is a function of the total configuration of employment arrangements. Research shows that there is a payoff between the quality of the entire configuration of employment arrangements in an organization and the presence of i-deals in this particular organization.

Using data of 3,427 organizations, Dorenbosch, van Zwieten, and Kraan (2012) showed that the level of standardization of employment arrangements (determined by union negotiations or collective labor agreements or negotiated within the organization) determines how large the zone for individual negotiations is. Innovative organizations with large numbers of highly educated employees reported more tailor-made arrangements regarding salaries, working times, and employee development. In addition, Kroon and Freese (2012) found that when the organizational climate for negotiating terms and conditions of employment was perceived to be more formalized, *the actual number of i-deals* dropped significantly. A remarkable finding was that when the climate for negotiating terms and conditions was perceived to be more innovative, the *number of requests for i-deals* dropped as well. This may indicate that when the organizational climate is reflected by flexibility, the need to *negotiate* i-deals reduces. In these cases, everyone's standard is customization.

The organizational climate (formalization versus innovation) can thus be seen as a seed for i-deal requests. An innovative organizational climate that allows flexibility and adaptability as a nature of HR policies may result in fewer requests for i-deals. The paradox is that, simultaneously, closing i-deals in a formalized culture may repair the lack of customization and thus is a sign of good people management. This may lead to the conclusion that the widespread presence of i-deals in the organization is an emergent form of HR failure, undermining formal HR policies (Fugate, 2012). When negotiating is part of the standard in the HR strategy (as in the innovative climate for employment conditions described by Kroon & Freese, 2012), i-deals can offer "secondary elastics" (Hornung, 2012) to a system of HR policies and practices designed to retain valued workers. Where the standard flexible employment conditions still do not match to individual requirements, i-deals can deliver additional customization. In a world where employee diversity is increasing rapidly, elasticity is badly needed to constitute employment relationships that are truly mutually beneficial to all employees. We therefore conclude that i-deals in the employment relationship is in worst cases a sign of repair and in best cases a sign of optimal customization taking place in the organization.

Benefits and costs of i-deals in employment relations

Before embracing the strategic choice to allow individually negotiated terms and conditions of employment to increase the secondary elastics in HRM, a critical review of costs and benefits of i-deals for different stakeholders in the organization is necessary. Below, we describe the costs and benefits of i-deals on the organizational, team, and individual levels based on SHRM theory, P–E fit theory, and empirical findings of i-deal research. This leads to an overview of conditions under which the strategic use of i-deals may work.

Organization

Benefits of i-deals for organizations from an SHRM perspective

The strategic use of i-deals, from an organization's perspective, follows from SHRM theories that focus on human capital as a unique tool to create competitive advantage, such as human capital theory (Becker, 1964; Flamholtz & Lacey, 1981) and the resource-based view (Barney, 1991). Human capital theory states that investments in employee skills and knowledge are owned by employees; when employees leave, their knowledge leaves with them. Especially when knowledge and skills are more company-specific, it will be harder to replace employees, which suggests that employee retention strategies need to be aimed most at those workers owning key human capital. In addition, the resource-based view holds that an organization can benefit from their human resources by deploying it as a rare, valuable, and inimitable source for competitive advantage of the firm. These perspectives provide guidance to questions as to which employees should be granted i-deals: in economic terms, it is more valuable for employers to invest in employment relationships by granting i-deals when human capital is rarer and more important for organization success (Lepak & Snell, 1999). Also, investing in good employment relations will facilitate the attraction of key talented employees. The theoretical claim that i-deals lead to attraction and retention of key employees by Hornung, Rousseau, and Glaser (2008) has hardly been investigated on the organizational level. Below, we summarize the contribution of i-deals to the main strategic outcomes for organizations: employee motivation and retention, organizational performance, talent development, and workforce employability.

Dorenbosch, Van Zwieten, and Kraan (2012) related the presence of i-deals in organizations to employee-related organization-level outcomes such as absenteeism, turnover, and performance. They demonstrated that tailor-made employment relations were positively related to organization performance and to reduced employee turnover and absence figures. Different types of i-deals were related to different outcomes, with i-deals about flexible work times relating positively to organization performance and reduced absenteeism and development i-deals relating to reduced employee turnover. However, financial i-deals (about salary and bonuses) related positively to employee turnover. It seems that the content of i-deals matters for organization-level outcomes.

Retention of talent is of particular importance for the continuity of organizations. "Talents" are employees who have been selected or appointed to take key positions, which differentially contribute to the organization's sustainable competitive advantage (Collings & Mellahi, 2009). People who are selected in the talent pool will typically participate in a training program, often associated with a number of trainee or assignment periods, mentoring, and remuneration schemes. However, these talents often are "high achievers" who may easily leave the pool to progress their careers as soon as the organization does not respond fast enough to their needs. I-deals could offer the secondary elastics on top of tailored, but still group-oriented, talent management programs. Indeed, Van Zijderveld and Sonnenberg (2012) found that people who were selected in talent pools had more development i-deals than "regular" employees. This indicates that managers recognize the market value of talents and are willing to grant requests to progress their careers. Moreover, employees who were granted i-deals reported higher levels of perceived fairness of their terms and conditions of employees than those who were not granted i-deals (Van Zijderveld & Sonnenberg, 2012). Although not tested in this research, fairness is known to increase employee retention (Colquitt, Conlon, Wesson, Porter, & Ng, 2001).

Another benefit of i-deals from an organizational perspective is a positive effect on workforce employability. Employability is the potential of employees to perform effectively in their current job, to find or create another job, and to optimally use their competencies at work (Van der Heijde & Van der Heijden, 2006). As employability tends to decrease with age (Schalk et al., 2010), it is often tied to the demographic changes in society. Because of the aging society, the demographic structure of many organizations is changing: the age of retirement is being delayed and the potential of younger workers is shrinking. It is beneficial for organizational continuity to take older worker's needs into consideration and keep them employable and productive during their entire career. The motives to stay in the workforce change when people grow older. In general, career growth ambitions reduce, while motives like having a meaningful job content increase (Kooij, de Lange, Jansen, & Dikkers, 2008). However, it is not recommendable to make one specific HR bundle for all older workers. Apart from the stigmatizing effect that such an approach may have, there is a sheer variation in motives and abilities among older workers. In another study, Kooij et al. found that four separate HR bundles can be applied to employ older workers (Kooij, Jansen, Dikkers, & Lange, 2014). In keeping older workers employed, managers need to understand the motives of their older workers and adjust the HR practices to their individual needs. These findings for older workers can be extended to other groups of employees who, for example, have care responsibilities for relatives or young children. In addition to initiatives to facilitate the combination of work and care for all employees (by offering flex hours or flex work places), in some cases special arrangements are needed to (temporarily) fit the requirements at work with the demands in the home environment (Ng & Feldman, 2008). Hence, i-deals can help to overcome personal issues due to age or home situation that inhibit employability, by adjusting individual work arrangements such that employees keep being able to do their current job or move to another job.

Costs of i-deals at the organizational level

The management of a system that allows every individual to negotiate their terms and conditions of employment brings additional *transaction costs* compared to systems that treat all employees equally, for example, in terms of coordinating and managing individualized employment packages (Marescaux, 2013). Transaction costs in HRM are those costs involved in making an economic exchange for labor. Firms strive for as minimum ex ante (making labor fit the requirements of the organization) and ex post (management) costs involved in managing the employment relationship (Williamson, 1975). The gains of an employment system involving the use of i-deals should be compared to the direct and indirect costs involved in maintaining such a system.

Direct costs involve negotiation and administrative tasks that will increase compared to standardized systems for terms and conditions of employment. Standardized HR policies are developed to distribute employee benefits in an efficient way. For instance, via collective labor agreements (CLAs), employees may not have to negotiate individually on their salary raises or the number of vacation days. These transactions costs are lower than in the case of i-deals, where each employee negotiates their own employment package with their supervisor. These arrangements have to be documented and checked, which lead to high transaction costs. So for reasons of efficiency, standardization of HR policies was designed at the expense of flexibility.

Indirect costs will follow from the need to communicate and ascertain *fairness* of each i-deal in the eyes of other employees doing similar jobs, as will be illustrated in the next section on team-level costs and benefits. Another source of indirect costs lies in making the HRM system *fit* with the institutional context of the organization, especially employment laws and CLAs, but also a company's existing culture may complicate (or facilitate) the use of i-deals.

Concluding: i-deals on organizational level

If we sum up the costs and benefits of i-deals at the organizational level, it can be concluded that i-deals bring in the potential of attracting, keeping, and motivating talented workers. Empirical evidence to corroborate these theoretical assumptions is scarce, and sometimes the relationship between the i-deal and the effect is contrary to what was expected. It appears that i-deals facilitate the career ambitions of high-achievers who are selected as talents to take future key positions in organizations. Moreover, research on interventions to increase the employability and vitality of older workers supports the need for individually tailored arrangements. Similarly, i-deals can facilitate the employability of workers with care responsibilities outside work. In most of these examples, the i-deals concern development or flexibility i-deals and special needs i-deals. The few findings on granting financial i-deals indicate that instead of keeping the employee, this may lead to higher turnover (Kroon & Freese, 2012). This raises questions on whether the intention of the i-deal is something positive to start with or is meant to repair an already damaged relationship (see also Chapter 3, this volume), which eventually does not lead to the intended result. As we demonstrated, the costs of introducing i-deals cannot be neglected and may not be necessary if the organizational climate is flexible and employment conditions are good. Severin Hornung refers to a U-shaped curve with respect to the trade-off between flexibility and standardization (Freese, Dorenbosch, & Kroon, 2012). Standardized HRM is characterized by rigidity, reducing a firm's potential to keep and motivate the best employees. On the other side of the curve stands an HR system that only relies on i-deals and which is characterized by chaos and high transaction costs.

Team level

When individuals negotiate i-deals, these result almost by definition is differential treatment within teams, triggering fairness evaluations among coworkers (Rousseau, Ho, & Greenberg, 2006). For i-deals to deliver the expected outcomes in terms of motivation and retention, it is important that coworkers are at the least not harmed by the i-deal, but even better when there are beneficial effects for others as well (Rousseau, 2005).

Benefits of i-deals for teams from an SHRM perspective

Although fairness and potential negative coworker reactions have drawn some research attention, positive outcomes of i-deals for teams are also likely. First of all, i-deals can be interpreted as a signal that the organization appreciates the needs of individual employees. When people in teams receive i-deals, coworkers could interpret this as a signal that there is room, in the future, to ask for personalized arrangements themselves (Lai, Rousseau, & Chang, 2009). This may evoke feelings of perceived organization support, which has been related to positive employee attitudes and behaviors (Eisenberger, Cummings, Armeli, & Lynch, 1997). This is more likely to happen when a team is informed or even involved in the creation of the i-deal. I-deals thus contribute to a perception of innovative employment arrangements, which was shown to have positive outcomes for individuals (Kroon & Freese, 2012).

Moreover, when there is room for individualized work arrangements, also people with special needs are enabled to work to their capacities. Personal care i-deals are special arrangements for employees needing extra care or attention because of their personal circumstances. For instance, personal care i-deals may allow chronically ill employees to work from home more often than other employees, to make sure that their energy levels are not affected too much by commuting. Or, they may allow single parents to start working later in the morning, so they can bring their children to school first. Scholars are beginning to address the topic of creating work environments where diverse individuals feel included. In inclusive groups, people are treated as insiders and also allowed/encouraged to retain uniqueness within the work group (Shore et al., 2010). I-deals can be used as an inclusiveness practice. Obviously, to let i-deals contribute to inclusiveness, it should be supported with a climate for inclusiveness and appropriate leadership styles (Shore et al., 2010). Perceptions of workgroup inclusion have positive outcomes for teams, as they can contribute to better understanding of each other and as such contribute to social relationships at work.

Costs of i-deals for teams

Some research has been executed on the consequences of introducing i-deals for coworkers, especially relating to fairness (see for instance Lai, Rousseau, & Chang, 2009). In this book, several chapters address the topic of i-deals and fairness and justice perceptions in teams (see e.g., Chapter 7 by Anand and Vidyarthi and Chapter 8 by Marescaux and De Winne, this volume).

Marescaux (2013) showed that the type of i-deal matters for coworker fairness perceptions. Financial i-deals lead to the strongest feelings of unfairness and the strongest reactions in terms of withholding effort and trying to counteract the i-deal. Under such circumstances, the contribution of the i-deal to satisfy the needs of one employee is cancelled out by negative responses and counterproductive behavior of coworkers.

Concluding: i-deals in teams

In teams where coworkers perceive that the procedures and distribution of i-deals are unfair, the costs resulting from demotivation and counterproductive performance of coworkers are likely to be higher than the benefits that may be present for the one employee who obtained the i-deal. However, when fairness is properly managed by means of fair regulations, communication, voice, and leadership, i-deals can contribute to perceived organization support and diversity-inclusive work teams. Furthermore, it seems that i-deals that accommodate how people can do their work (working times, personal care, development) are more easily accepted in teams than financial i-deals.

Employee level

The primary focus of the benefits of i-deals is at the level of the individual worker. The assumption is that because the employment conditions better fit the individual's needs, this eventually leads to positive effects for the organization, through higher motivation to contribute to the organization and a lower intention to leave the organization (Hornung et al., 2008; Rousseau, 2005). Through customization of working conditions to employee characteristics such as skills, interests, needs, talents, or performance, valuable employees can be attracted, motivated, and retained, sustaining organizational performance (Rousseau, 2005).

Benefits of i-deals on the employee level: different i-deals, different outcomes

Although research on i-deals indeed shows positive effects of i-deals on the individual level, it also suggests a more complex relationship between i-deals and motivation and retention. Only under certain conditions or for certain groups of workers, some kinds of i-deals show positive effects for motivation and retention. Flexibility i-deals are related to lower work–family conflict (Hornung et al., 2008) and are positively related to the motivation of older workers to keep on working after retirement (Bal, De Jong, Jansen & Bakker, 2012). Development i-deals are related to higher performance expectations, higher organizational commitment (Hornung et al., 2008), and organizational citizenship behavior for low-quality relationships at work (Anand, Vidyarthi, Liden, Robert, & Rousseau, 2010). In a study by Kroon and Freese (2012) however, positive effects were only found when employees reported that their i-deal was beneficial for both the organization and themselves. In case the i-deal was beneficial for one party only, negative effects of i-deals were found: higher turnover intentions and lower satisfaction with employment conditions. They also found that workers with a financial i-deal are less engaged and display lower levels of organizational citizenship behavior. What these findings show is that it matters which kinds of i-deals are offered; some i-deals are more favorable for organizational performance than others. Developmental i-deals seem to have more direct links with organizational performance than the other kinds of i-deals. Moreover, some effects are only revealed indirectly and in the long run. Workers with lower work–family conflict could be less likely to resign or stay working for more hours than workers who do experience work–family conflict. These possible, long-term effects only form a mild support for the introduction of i-deals in the organization.

Costs of i-deals on the employee level

Notwithstanding the beneficial outcomes for the individual, some harmful side effects may happen for employees who negotiated an i-deal for themselves. Fugate (2012) warned that when an i-deal is explained as a "special treatment," this could alienate or stigmatize employees in their work groups. Instead of inclusion, it could lead to excluding an employee to optimally contribute in a team (Shore et al., 2010). Moreover, when i-deals result in very high levels of psychological contract uniqueness, employees may become too tied to the organization and see little value in moving to another job. Such arrangements hinder employability and mobility of employees.

Another concern involves the negotiation process leading to an i-deal. When employees request an i-deal and this i-deal is denied, they may be disappointed about the organization. Kroon and Freese (2012) found that requesting i-deals, but not receiving them, has more negative effects for satisfaction and retention than simply not having an i-deal. Likewise, not all employees have equal negotiation power. There is the risk that only workers with high negotiation skills or a strong position in the labor market are able to close i-deals, potentially leading to the "Matthew effect"; the rich get richer and the poor get poorer.

Concluding: i-deals on the employee level

There appear to be obvious dark sides to granting i-deals, also on the individual level, where i-deals are assumed to have the most positive effects. Observing the costs and benefits of i-deals, it appears that for i-deals to contribute to desired outcomes, they need to be carefully managed.

Effective management of i-deals

Introducing i-deals has costs and benefits. To reap the benefits, i-deals in organizations must be carefully managed. This implies that we no longer should look at i-deals as a potential side effect from incidental requests for customization, which are tacitly granted by managers in the organization. Instead, i-deals must be regarded as an integral part of the HR strategy of the organization, and a strategic choice has to be made, to establish why, when, and how i-deals can be part of the total employment package. Again, management action is required on various levels in the organization.

Strategic choice: standardization and flexibility

The strategic choice to add i-deals as an HR practice to optimize fit between individual needs and their job requirements depends on a number of considerations. First, the choice about the balance between standardization and flexibility in employment arrangements is inevitably contextually bound. The flexibility or rigidity of the HR system is bounded by the zone of negotiation left after taking employment laws and CLAs into account. CLAs are often referred to by HR managers as severely reducing flexibility in the HR system. On the other hand, CLAs offer protection to weaker groups in the labor market, who may not have the power to negotiate their terms and conditions (Bidwell et al., 2013). In addition, strong works councils may reduce individual negotiations on i-deals. However, if the standardized employment arrangements are generous and allow need fulfillment of diverse groups in the organization, the need for i-deal closing may be low to start with.

Second, the HR strategy should set the goal for introducing i-deals in the organization. What is the main objective for i-deal initiatives? Is it to enhance employability of senior employees, to attract young talented workers, or to repair unintended injustice which can be part of standardized HR policies? In his column Fugate (2012) states "To optimize resources, employers and HR managers need to identify which i-deals initiatives are most valued by the targeted employees, rather than simply providing common or 'off-the-shelf' practices (e.g., common forms of training and generic schedule flexibility). Next, determine which of those identified can feasibly be provided, given financial, regulatory, and other constraints." In this phase, the rules of the game are set. It involves a strategic discussion on for which purpose and under which conditions i-deals are part of the HR policies.

Third, the transaction costs involved in customizing employment arrangements to individuals need consideration. In a reflection on optimizing the pay off between customization benefits and costs, Boudreau suggested taking a marketing perspective (Freese et al., 2012). When looking for the optimal payoff between standardization and customization, marketeers use a market-segmentation approach: they examine which groups with distinct needs can be discerned and suggest product differentiations that fit with the needs of each group. In this way, they manage customization without losing volume and without increasing production costs beyond sales benefits. In the case of i-deals, the sales benefits are the costs involved in replacing valuable employees who would otherwise leave the organization when the organization would not respond to their individual needs. Production costs are the costs involved in making arrangements to realize the i-deal, such as investing in (computer) equipment, rescheduling teamwork, training costs, and the like. Although in theory each employee is unique, it is possible to define groups with similar needs in organizations (Jackson et al., 2013). By segmenting employees into groups with similar needs, particular HR practices can be developed to address their needs without the need to make large investments in single i-deals for each individual employee. This seems a fruitful approach to balancing standardization and tailoring employment arrangements. Moreover, such an approach would help to define rules and policies that in turn will contribute to a better acceptance of i-deals. In fact, this approach can be found in practice. A study by Freese et al. (2012) in 39 organizations indicates that knowledge workers or high-skilled production workers with an open-ended contract are granted all kinds of i-deals, with the aim of retention. Contractors with highly specialized skills are granted financial i-deals, to develop a long-term relationship. Noncore workers with a permanent employment contract can negotiate development i-deals to stimulate internal and external mobility. Finally, low-skilled workers on temporary contracts performing routine tasks (call center employees, for instance), do not get any i-deals at all.

Fourth, since i-deals involve employee negotiations with their supervisors, a supportive negotiation culture is necessary. The degree of formalization in the organization plays a key role, as a lot of rules, procedures, and structures constrains the willingness and ability of supervisors to create differentiation (Rousseau, 2005). HR managers mention that line managers often use the words "impossible, because HR does not allow i-deals" when employees pose a request for a personalized arrangement (Freese et al., 2012). Moreover, the organizational culture determines the degree to which the organization promotes HR differentiation. Highly innovative and supportive work cultures will have a higher degree of flexibility to individualize working conditions because they implement fewer rules, procedures, and structures (Rousseau, 2005). Bureaucratic work cultures focusing on efficiency will have a lot of rules, procedures, and structures in place, reducing the degree of flexibility to differentiate in working conditions. This will reflect in the perceived climate for negotiations (Kroon & Freese, 2012). Hence, the climate for employment negotiations (innovative, or formal and bureaucratic) contributes to the likelihood that i-deal negotiations will be initiated by employees and agreed upon by managers.

Fifth, the concern that only workers with high negotiation skills or a strong position in the labor market are able to close i-deals (potentially leading to the "Matthew effect") must be counteracted by identifying employees that are not able to effectively negotiate i-deals. Training or mentoring for these groups and awareness for this side effect by management is necessary.

Finally, there is a clear need to manage the indirect costs that follow from using i-deals: fairness issues, organization climate, and tacit leadership issues interfere with its effectiveness. In a study with 39 HR directors of preferred employers in The Netherlands, Freese et al. (2012) found that there was a great reluctance to introduce i-deals as part of the HR policies in the organization because of a concern for unequal treatment of employees. At the same time, most acknowledged that i-deals were granted by supervisors, tacitly. As our review illustrates, tacit and unmanaged i-deals may have more harmful side effects than when clear policies are in place. Moreover, the execution of these policies needs strong managers. This latter point refers to the role of line managers in effectively dealing with i-deals.

Line managers' role in i-deal management

I-deals pose a dilemma to HR managers. Consistency is an important element in a procedurally fair HR system, but some degree of flexibility is needed to adapt to changing circumstances. Yet, inconsistent HR practices can erode trust and motivation. Rousseau (2005, p. 193) addresses this dilemma as follows: "This tension between consistency and flexibility is not a problem to solve, but a fact to be managed."

Supervisors are organizational agents that need to balance the interests of the individual worker and the interests of the organization. They are the ones in charge of implementing HR practices and have the power to grant requests for differentiation (Hornung et al., 2009). In the study by Freese et al. (2012), the HR directors referred to the necessity of strong leadership to be able to negotiate successful i-deals. Granting i-deals implies that leaders dare to differentiate between employees. It is not about treating employees equally, it is about treating employees fairly. An important principle to fairly introduce i-deals is that managers must believe it is in the organization's best interest to grant the i-deal requested by the employee. Managers are supposed to act in the organization's best interest and if the i-deal meets this criterion, explaining the i-deal to other team members is possible. Transparency is essential for perceptions of organizational justice. Procedural justice implies that decisions with regard to granting i-deals are free from bias, based on correct and accurate information, consistent, and meet ethical standards (Leventhal, 1976). If these criteria are met, i-deal decisions can be shared with all team members and they can raise their voice to adjust possibly bad outcomes of the i-deal. In her book, Rousseau (2005) described a manager who always responded to an employee requesting an i-deal: "Tell me why it is legitimate." When employees have clear *line of sight* on the goals of the team and the organization, they will be able to link their needs to the requirements of the organization (Boswell, 2006). In this way, individual requests for employment arrangements can be aligned with the greater benefit of the organization (vertical fit), which will also facilitate communication and acceptance by other stakeholders in the organization.

Conclusion

The central issue addressed in this chapter concerned the potential of i-deals to be part of an HRM strategy that contributes to the needs and goals of organizations, teams, and individual employees alike. Because i-deals concern a specific type of customization within employment relationships, we first outlined various elements of customization of employment terms and conditions at different levels in the employment relationship. I-deals are the ultimate form of customized employment arrangements, which come on top of differentiated (group) deals and unique organization-level arrangements.

The literature review zoomed in on costs and benefits involved in i-deals for organizations, teams, and individual employees. The scarce literature on the outcomes of i-deals at the level of organizations indicates that different types of i-deals hold different outcomes for employee motivation and retention. While the use of flexibility and development i-deals in organizations relates positively to organization performance, financial i-deals seem to hold negative relations with organization performance. From an organization perspective, it appears that i-deals are particularly beneficial to enhance employability and retention of older workers, parents, and "talents." At the team level, coworkers of i-dealers are most directly confronted with the consequences of i-deals. A keen management and clear communication to "third parties" is deemed necessary, to avoid feeling of unfairness among coworkers. Again, financial i-deals seem to yield the strongest feelings of injustice. Finally, the largest benefits of i-deals are generally expected at the individual employee level. However, studies also reveal potential harmful side effects that may happen when employees are denied an i-deal or when an i-deal leads to the stigmatization of an employee.

Given that not all outcomes of i-deals are straightforwardly beneficial to organizations, teams, or individual employees, conditions for effective i-deals need to be taken into account. These are the regulatory context, the HR strategy vision and communication on individualized employment arrangements, the HR climate for flexible employment arrangement negotiations, the transaction costs involved in managing i-deals, and an awareness of the negotiation power of employee groups to avoid exclusion of weaker employee groups (women, older workers, minorities). In practice, effective management of i-deals will require strong leadership of line managers. Their skills to be transparent about differentiating between employees and involving employees to see how differentiation contributes to the benefit of all in the organization will facilitate the use of i-deals by those individuals who need it to optimize person–organization fit.

To conclude, i-deals can only be an effective part of strategic HRM if a deliberate choice is made about which strategic goal is served by introducing i-deals in the organization. It must be clear under which conditions i-deals are acceptable as part of the employment relationship. A supportive negotiation climate and strong leadership that is able to transparently discuss i-deals in work groups are essential.

Note

1 Brigitte Kroon, Charissa Freese, and René Schalk, Tilburg University, the Netherlands.

References

Anand, S., Vidyarthi, P.R., Liden, R.C., & Rousseau, D.M. (2010). Good citizens in poor-quality relationships: Idiosyncratic deals as a substitute for relationship quality. *Academy of Management Journal, 53*(5), 970–988.

Arthur, J.B., & Boyles, T. (2007). Validating the human resource system structure: A levels-based strategic HRM approach. *Human Resource Management Review, 17*(1), 77–92. doi:10.1016/j.hrmr.2007.02.001

Bal, P.M., De Jong, S.B., Jansen, P.G., & Bakker, A.B. (2012). Motivating employees to work beyond retirement: A multi-level study of the role of i-deals and unit climate. *Journal of Management Studies, 49*(2), 306–331.

Barney, J. (1991). Firm resources and sustained competitive advantage. *Journal of Management, 17*(1), 99–120.

Becker, B.E., & Huselid, M.A. (2006). Strategic human resources management: Where do we go from here? *Journal of Management, 32*(6), 898–925. doi:10.1177/0149206306293668

Becker, G.S. (1964). *Human capital* (2nd ed.). New York: Columbia University Press.

Bidwell, M., Briscoe, F., Fernandez-Mateo, I., & Sterling, A. (2013). The employment relationship and inequality: How and why changes in employment practices are reshaping rewards in organizations. *Academy of Management Annals, 7*(1), 61–121. doi:10.1080/19416520.2013.761403

Boswell, W. (2006). Aligning employees with the organization's strategic objectives: Out of "line of sight", out of mind. *International Journal of Human Resource Management, 17*(9), 1489–1511. doi:10.1080/09585190600878071

Boxall, P., & Purcell, J. (2008). *Strategy and human resource management* (3rd ed., p. 408). New York: Palgrave Macmillan.

Clinton, M., & Guest, D. (2013). Testing universalistic and contingency HRM assumptions across job levels. *Personnel Review, 42*(5), 529–551. doi:10.1108/PR-07-2011-0109

Collings, D.G., & Mellahi, K. (2009). Strategic talent management: A review and research agenda. *Human Resource Management Review, 19*(4), 304–313.

Colquitt, J.A., Conlon, D.E., Wesson, M.J., Porter, C.O.L.H., & Ng, K.Y. (2001). Justice at the millenium: A meta-analytic review of 25 years of organizational justice research. *Journal of Applied Psychology, 86*(3), 425–445. doi:10.1037//0021–9010.86.3.425

Delery, J.E. (1998). Issues of fit in strategic human resource management: Implications for research. *Human Resource Management Review, 8*(3), 289–309.

Dorenbosch, L., Van Zwieten, M., & Kraan, K. (2012). I-deals in Nederland: Welke werkgevers sluiten ze en wat kan het hun opleveren? [I-deals in the Netherlands: Use and benefits for employers]. *Tijdschrift Voor HRM, 15*(2), 14–36.

Eisenberger, R., Cummings, J., Armeli, S., & Lynch, P. (1997). Perceived organizational support, discretionary treatment, and job satisfaction. *Journal of Applied Psychology, 82*(5), 812–20. Retrieved from http://www.ncbi.nlm.nih.gov/pubmed/9337610

Flamholtz, E.G., & Lacey, J.M. (1981). *Personnel management, human capital theory, and human resource accounting*. Los Angeles: Institute of Industrial Relations, University of California.

Freese, C., Dorenbosch, L., & Kroon, B. (2012). Strategic HR and proactive employees. Managing job crafters and proactive employees: a blessing or nightmare for HRM? In *Panel Symposium AOM* (pp. 1–7). Boston.

Fugate, M. (2012). Being strategic about idiosyncratic deals and employability. *Tijdschrift Voor HRM, 15*(2), 77–78.

Gerhart, B. (2007). Horizontal and vertical fit in human resource systems. In C. Ostroff (Ed.), *Perspectives on organizational fit* (pp. 317–418). London: Taylor & Francis Group.

Guest, D. (2002). Human resource management, corporate performance and employee well-being: Building the worker into HRM. *Journal of Industrial Relations, 44*(3), 335–358.

Hornung, S. (2012). Employee responses to work design: Integrating the job demands–resources model and self-determination theory. *International Journal of Psychology, 47*(January), p. 501.

Hornung, S., Rousseau, D.M., & Glaser, J. (2008). Creating flexible work arrangements through idiosyncratic deals. *Journal of Applied Psychology, 93*(3), 655–664. doi:10.1037/0021-9010.93.3.655

Hornung, S., Rousseau, D.M., & Glaser, J. (2009). Why supervisors make idiosyncratic deals: Antecedents and outcomes of i-deals from a managerial perspective. *Journal of Managerial Psychology, 24*(8), 738–764. doi:10.1108/02683940910996770

Huselid, M.A. (1995). The impact of human resource management practices on turnover, productivity and corporate financial performance. *Academy of Management Journal, 38*(3), 635–672.

Jackson, S.E., Schuler, R.S., & Jiang, K. (2013, July). An aspirational framework for strategic human resource management. *Academy of Management Annals*, 1–89. doi:10.1080/19416520.2014.872335

Jiang, K., Lepak, D.P., Han, K., Hong, Y., Kim, A., & Winkler, A.-L. (2012). Clarifying the construct of human resource systems: Relating human resource management to employee performance. *Human Resource Management Review, 22*(2), 73–85. doi:10.1016/j.hrmr.2011.11.005

Kooij, D., de Lange, A., Jansen, P., & Dikkers, J. (2008). Older workers' motivation to continue to work: Five meanings of age: A conceptual review. *Journal of Managerial Psychology, 23*(4), 364–394.

Kooij, D.T.A.M., Jansen, P.G.W., Dikkers, J.S.E., & de Lange, A.H. (2014). Managing aging workers: A mixed methods study on bundles of HR practices for aging workers. *International Journal of Human Resource Management, 25*(15), 2192–2212. Retrieved from http://www.tandfonline.com/doi/pdf/10.1080/09585192.2013.872169

Kroon, B., & Freese, C. (2012). Dragen i-deals bij aan motivatie en behoud van werknemers? *Tijdschrift Voor HRM, 15*(2), 43–58.

Lai, L., Rousseau, D.M., & Chang, K.T.T. (2009). Idiosyncratic deals: Coworkers as interested third parties. *Journal of Applied Psychology, 94*(2), 547–556. doi:10.1037/a0013506

Lengnick-Hall, M.L., Lengnick-Hall, C.A., Andrade, L.S., & Drake, B. (2009). Strategic human resource management: The evolution of the field. *Human Resource Management Review, 19*(2), 64–85. doi:10.1016/j.hrmr.2009.01.002

Lepak, D.P., & Snell, S.A. (1999). The human resource architecture: Toward a theory of human capital allocation and development. *Academy of Management Review, 24*(1), 31–48.

Leventhal, G.S. (1976). The distribution of rewards and resources in groups and organizations. *Advances in Experimental Social Psychology, 9*, 91–131.

Macduffie, J.P. (1995). Human resource bundles and manufacturing performance: Organizational logic and flexible production systems in the world auto industry. *Industrial and Labor Relations Review, 48*(2), 197–221.

Marescaux, E. (2013). *The impact of HR differentiation on employees*. Leuven: Faculteit Economie en Bedrijfswetenschappen, KU Leuven.

Ng, T.W.H., & Feldman, D.C. (2008). Can you get a better deal elsewhere? The effects of psychological contract replicability on organizational commitment over time. *Journal of Vocational Behavior, 73*(2), 268–277. doi:10.1016/j.jvb.2008.05.004

Ostroff, C., & Schulte, M. (2007). Multiple perspectives of fit in organization across levels of analysis. In C. Ostroff & T.A. Judge (Eds.), *Perspectives on organizational fit* (pp. 3–70). London: Taylor & Francis Group.

Rosen, C.C., Slater, D.J., Chang, C.-H., & Johnson, R.E. (2011). Let's make a deal: Development and validation of the ex post i-deals scale. *Journal of Management, 39*(3), 709–742. doi:10.1177/0149206310394865

Rousseau, D.M. (2005). *I-deals: Idiosyncratic deals employees bargain for themselves*. Armonk, NY: M.E. Sharpe.

Rousseau, D.M., Ho, V.T., & Greenberg, J. (2006). I-deals: Idiosyncratic terms in employment relationships. *Academy of Management Review, 31*, 977–994.

Schalk, R., Van Veldhoven, M., De Lange, A.H., De Witte, H., Kraus, K., Stamov-Rossnagel, C., . . . , & Zacher, H. (2010). Moving European research on work and ageing forward: Overview and agenda. *European Journal of Work and Organizational Psychology, 19*(1), 76–101.

Shore, L.M., Randel, A.E., Chung, B.G., Dean, M.A., Holcombe Ehrhart, K., & Singh, G. (2010). Inclusion and diversity in work groups: A review and model for future research. *Journal of Management, 37*(4), 1262–1289. doi:10.1177/0149206310385943

Van der Heijde, C.M., & Van der Heijden, B.I. (2006). A competence-based and multidimensional operationalization and measurement of employability. *Human Resource Management, 45*(3), 449–476.

Van Zijderveld, V., & Sonnenberg, M. (2012). I-deals en rechtvaardigheid: Het effect van talent differentiatie [I-deals and fairness: Consequenses of talent differentiation]. *Tijdschrift Voor HRM, 15*(2), 61–76.

Williamson, O.E. (1975). Markets and hierarchies. *American Economic Review, 63*, 316–325.

Wright, P.M., Dunford, B.B., & Snell, S.A. (2001). Human resources and the resource based view of the firm. *Journal of Management, 27*(6), 701–721. doi:10.1177/014920630102700607

Wright, P.M., & Nishii, L.H. (2007). *Strategic HRM and organizational behavior: Integrating multiple levels of analysis*. Ithaca, NY: CAHRS Working Paper Series.

Wrzesniewski, A., & Dutton, J.E. (2001). Crafting a job: Revisioning employees as active crafters of their work, *26*(2), 179–201.

7
IDIOSYNCRATIC DEALS IN THE CONTEXT OF WORKGROUPS

Smriti Anand and Prajya Vidyarthi[1]

Introduction

Employees are no longer passive recipients of standardized or one-size-fits-all terms of employment arrangements; they actively shape their working conditions to suit their personal needs, wants, and aspirations. These customized employment arrangements, also termed idiosyncratic deals (i-deals; Rousseau, 2005), comprise employees negotiating various valuable and meaningful aspects of their employment, such as work schedule or career growth opportunities, with the intent to improve the quality of their on- and off-the-job life. Such individualized work arrangements are increasingly becoming common due to the new reality of the employment relationship (Coyle-Shapiro, Shore, Taylor, & Tetrick, 2004), whereby instead of lifelong employment, employees look for and demand opportunities to increase their employability and to fulfill their lives. I-deals theory adds a new perspective to the existing theories of employment relationship (e.g., Morrison & Robinson, 1997) and job design (Grant & Parker, 2009). For example, i-deals theory bridges and builds upon two dominant but inherently divergent approaches of work design, namely top-down management-initiated interventions geared to make a class of jobs more intrinsically motivating (Hackman & Oldham, 1980) and bottom-up efforts from employees to redefine their job roles and duties without formal authorization from the employer (Wrzesniewski & Dutton, 2001). The increasing prevalence of i-deals in management practice (Lawler & Finegold, 2000) combined with their strong implications for employee recruitment, retention, and satisfaction (Capelli, 2000) makes this an important area of research in the management literature.

In this chapter, we review developments in i-deals research since the inception of this theory. This review is based on empirical as well as theory papers cited in social sciences indexes since 2001. Until now, scholars have largely examined i-deals as if they occur in a vacuum. However, Rousseau's initial conceptualization of i-deals (Greenberg, Roberge, Ho, & Rousseau, 2004; Rousseau, 2001, 2005) suggests that leaders and coworkers are the other two parties to any i-deals formed by a group member. Leaders personify the organization and also tend to be the primary grantors of i-deals. Coworkers provide support and can be the enablers of other group members' i-deals. Therefore, this review begins by exploring the relationship between leadership and i-deals. Next we examine how the workgroup attributes set boundaries to this relationship. Finally, we end this review by discussing how the distribution of i-deals among group members can create within-group differences, and how those differences can affect outcomes for the entire team.

Antecedents of i-deals: the role of leaders

Leaders play an important role in negotiating and implementing any i-deals. They tend to be the authority figure to whom employees go to negotiate i-deals. Even when leaders do not have the complete authority to grant i-deals, the decision makers seek their input. Extant research has explored the relationship between leadership and i-deals primarily at the individual employee's level. For example, the effect of dyadic relationship quality between the employee and the leader has been investigated in a number of studies (e.g., Rosen, Slater, Chang, & Johnson, 2013). Research has also examined the effect of leader's consideration on an individual's i-deals (Hornung, Rousseau, Glaser, Angerer, & Weigl, 2011). However, these studies have by and large ignored the workgroup in which the dyadic relationships exist. In this section, we first review existing research on leadership and i-deals, and then make propositions to explore these relationships at multiple levels, such as individual within the group, or meso, and group level.

Leader–member exchange (LMX) and i-deals

I-deal scholars maintain that employees are more likely to seek and get i-deals when they are in a high-quality exchange relationship with their leaders (e.g., Hornung, Rousseau, Weigl, Müller, & Glaser, 2014). Empirical studies have shown that in comparison to employees' individual attributes such as political skills, LMX is a stronger predictor of i-deals (Rosen et al., 2013). Research has also shown that LMX can set boundaries to the effects of i-deals (Anand, Vidyarthi, Liden, & Rousseau, 2010). LMX theory is based on the premise that leaders differentiate between their subordinates such that only a few enjoy a high-quality relationship with the leader (Liden & Graen, 1980). However, empirical research on i-deals has treated LMX relationships as if they exist in a vacuum. It behooves future researchers to explore the relationship between LMX and i-deals at multiple levels of theory by taking the workgroup context in account. The LMX to i-deals relationship can be explored at the meso level by looking at an individual's relative LMX (LMX with respect to the average of the group) and at the group level by looking at LMX differentiation, i.e., the extent to which a leader differentiates between group members in terms of LMX quality.

Relative LMX and i-deals

According to LMX theory, leaders establish high-quality relationships with some subordinates and lower quality ones with the others. High LMX relationships are based on social exchange, whereas the low-quality ones are driven by transactional exchange. High LMX relationships are associated with mutual respect, negotiability, and various rewards (Liden & Graen, 1980). The majority of research has explored LMX at the individual employee's level; however, a few scholars have examined LMX through the lens of individual-within-group theory (e.g., Schriesheim, Castro, Zhou, & Yammarino, 2001). In this tradition, within-group relative LMX quality, or relative LMX (RLMX), is defined as an individual's LMX in comparison to the average level of LMX in the workgroup. Scholars have empirically demonstrated that RLMX can explain additional variance in outcomes beyond that explained by LMX (Henderson, Wayne, Shore, Bommer, & Tetrick, 2008). We propose that an individual's RLMX quality may correspond to the likelihood of negotiating an i-deal, which is a scarce resource, just as there tend to be few high LMX relationships within a workgroup (Liden, Erdogan, Wayne, & Sparrowe, 2006; Liden & Graen, 1980).

I-deals can be negotiated between an employee and a wide array of organizational representatives, such as the HR personnel and workgroup managers. Managers personify the organization (Shore et al., 2004), and particularly in the case of i-deals they may be largely responsible for managing those, therefore employees are most likely to negotiate any deals with their immediate managers (Rousseau, 2005). Further, because the numerous benefits of a high LMX relationship include higher negotiability, employees with high LMX are more likely to perceive availability of i-deals. Extending this line of reasoning to account for the workgroup context, we assert that the perceptions of i-deal availability driven by social comparison processes occurring at the individual-within-group level will account for the relationship between RLMX and i-deals, beyond what is explained by individual-level perceptions of LMX.

> Proposition 1: Relative LMX is positively related to i-deals, while controlling for individual-level perceptions of LMX.

Relative LMX and i-deals: moderating effect of LMX differentiation

LMX theory asserts that leaders employ differentiation to more efficiently allocate their scarce time and resources to a few trusted subordinates. Members in high LMX relationships enjoy tangible and intangible rewards, which are not available to those with low quality LMX (Graen & Uhl-Bien, 1995). Though all managers engage in LMX differentiation, there is variability in its extent. Thus, workgroups vary in the extent of differences between members' LMXs (e.g., Liden et al., 2006). Some managers may have a fairly uniform level of relationship quality with each member of the group (i.e., low LMX differentiation), whereas some others may have a small in-group and larger out-group of members. In a group with high LMX differentiation, members with high RLMX (i.e., closeness to the leader relative to peers) are likely to gain more advantages from the leader in comparison to their counterparts with low RLMX. Also, the nature of social comparison (Festinger, 1954) suggests that comparison of advantages, resulting from one's relative quality of LMX, is likely to be more favorable in a workgroup with higher extent of differentiation.

The advantages of high RLMX are likely to diminish when many group members have high-quality relationships with the leader. These groups are characterized by an overall positive tone of relationship, and leaders may be inclined to provide fairly equal treatment to all members in order to maintain social harmony (e.g., Hooper & Martin, 2008). Also, a leader has only a finite amount of resources to distribute amongst the entire group. Though the subordinates with high RLMX are likely to get a bigger share of these resources, if there are many of them, each person gets a smaller share in comparison to members in a workgroup with a higher degree of LMX differentiation. In groups with high LMX differentiation, there are few members with high RLMX, and therefore leader's rewards are distributed amongst few, rather than many, resulting in bigger advantage for each individual. Thus, high RLMX is likely to yield enhanced rewards for members in groups with higher rather than lower LMX differentiation.

Proposition 2: LMX differentiation will moderate the relationship between relative LMX and i-deals such that the relationship will be stronger in groups with high LMX differentiation.

Leadership style and i-deals

I-deals are sought to fulfill employees' unique needs and desires, so it is likely that employees tend to negotiate when they perceive their leader to be a considerate person. Indeed, Hornung and colleagues (2011) found support for this notion in an empirical study. These researchers found that employees are more likely to negotiate for i-deals when they perceive a people-oriented rather than task-oriented leader who is considerate of their personal needs. More insights can be gained by looking at how other leader attitudes and behaviors, such as demonstrating openness to making i-deals and fairness, influence i-deals for the workgroup members.

Leader openness and i-deals

I-deal negotiations are likely to be stifled before they start if the leader shows no openness to customization of work arrangements. Initiating an i-deal negotiation is a display of proactive behavior on the employee's part (Hornung, Rousseau, & Glaser, 2008). This proactivity is motivated by the desire to enhance the quality of one's work environment. The i-deal negotiating employee faces the risk of negotiation failure resulting in the denial of the i-deal; that is, not getting the special employment arrangements asked for. If the negotiation fails, the employee stands to lose face and yet needs to continue to work in the same workgroup. In order to mitigate this risk, employees may go through considerable preparation before proposing an i-deal. Employees carefully observe their surroundings (leaders, coworkers, general environment, etc.) and then decide the content, timing, and process of the negotiation before making any proposals (Rousseau, 2005).

Even when the leader is not the primary grantor of i-deals, her approval and support might be key to a successful negotiation. If the HR manager or the work unit head (i.e., high-level manager) has the authority to grant deals, they are likely to seek the leader's (i.e., the immediate manager's) input to understand all the involved issues, such as the negotiating individual's past and current performance, any past psychological contract breaches requiring amends, project schedules and deadlines, and other relevant circumstances for the entire workgroup. It would also be difficult, if not impossible, to implement any deals without the leader's support. Having customized work arrangements for even one member increases the leader's burden in terms of coordination and control of tasks between all the workgroup members. Finally, the leader's attitudes set the tone for the entire workgroup (Sy, Côté, & Saavedra, 2005), so his/her openness to i-deals can create a supportive ambience for any potential i-deal negotiators. Therefore, the employees are likely to be quite motivated to understand their leader's attitude towards any sort of i-deal that creates different terms of employment in the same workgroup.

Leaders might be open to customization for a number of reasons. They might believe the deals to be a tool for employee recruitment, motivation, and retention. Some leaders may consider i-deals to be testing grounds for incremental changes and eventual policy making. Many others might be Theory Y managers who believe in creating an environment conducive to employee development by granting more autonomy and flexibility to their subordinates. Employees can sense their leader's openness to i-deals in multiple ways. First, the leader's track record of granting i-deals can be a sign of openness to future deals. Second, the leader might express positive views about customization of work arrangements in formal and informal communications. A leader who says that customized developmental opportunities increase employee satisfaction and also enhance performance is likely to be open to customization of job assignments, so that employees can proceed toward fulfillment of their professional aspirations. Finally, nothing says it better than the leader himself having an i-deal. The leader's i-deal legitimizes the concept for the rest of the workgroup. The leader's work-schedule flexibility i-deal sends a powerful message to the employees about the legitimacy and acceptance of work-schedule customization to engender work–life balance. In such a group, employees are likely to negotiate and get not only flexibility but also other types of i-deals.

> *Proposition 3: Employees are more likely to negotiate i-deals when the leader demonstrates openness to making i-deals.*

Leader fairness and i-deals

I-deals represent a departure from existing policies and standard work arrangements and thus run the risk of being considered unfair (Rousseau, Ho, & Greenberg, 2006).

Whether a deal is deemed unfair by one's colleagues depends largely on how the deal was granted. In an empirical study, Lai, Rousseau, and Chang (2009) found that group members are more willing to accept a colleague's i-deal when the underlying criteria are perceived to be fair. Because leaders tend to be the primary grantors of any i-deals, their reputation for fairness is likely to shape the workgroup's perceptions of fairness regarding any i-deals. We, therefore, assert that employees are more likely to seek an i-deal from a fair leader and avoid creating perceptions of unfairness in their colleagues. Employees perceive interactional fairness from their leader when they are treated respectfully and are provided with explanations for decisions (Bies & Moag, 1986). These perceptions are discussed amongst group members and create a shared perception of the leader's fairness in interactions with the employees (e.g., Simons & Roberson, 2003). Group members care not only about their own treatment from the leader, but also about that granted to their colleagues (Colquitt, 2004). There is some evidence that coworkers' perceptions can influence the extent to which i-deals are prevalent in a workgroup (Lai et al., 2009). Members of a workgroup led by a fair manager are more likely to believe they can make customized arrangements without the stigma of unfairness. On the other hand, employee perceptions about the possibility of fairly negotiated customized arrangements may diminish if most group members perceive their manager to be unjust. In this scenario, an i-deal may look like a device to further undermine the group justice climate, thus discouraging group members from making any personalized arrangements.

Fairly negotiated deals are also likely to come from a leader who is fair in implementing the organization's policies and procedures. Although the procedures and policies are created by the organization, it is the leader who applies them. Procedural fairness is demonstrated by being consistent and unbiased across workgroup members in applying procedures and policies, after gathering all appropriate information and taking all parties' interests into consideration (Leventhal, 1980). The leader's reputation for being procedurally fair signals fairness of procedures used to allocate rewards. These perceptions of fairness indicate that the leader allows negotiation of unique deals to meet individual needs only when fairness of procedures is maintained. The leader's procedural fairness also indicates her/his consistency in applying procedures, therefore a deal recipient's coworkers can also negotiate an i-deal by following the same procedures. For example, if the organization's policy demands an 8-hour-long work day, any employee can negotiate to start later or earlier and still maintain the 8-hour day. The leader may also demand evidence of need for flexibility from anyone who chooses to negotiate. Consistent and open procedures and communication remove any mysterious aspects of an i-deal. Thus, when the leader is considered fair, the i-deal recipient's coworkers are less likely to perceive unfairness in a deal. By mitigating workgroup perceptions of unfairness of i-deals, the leader's fairness reputation may encourage more group members to make i-deals geared to fulfill their individual needs.

> *Proposition 4: Employees are more likely to negotiate i-deals when the workgroup perceives the leader to be fair.*

Leadership style and i-deals: moderating effect of workgroup attributes

Though leaders are the primary grantors of any i-deals, they do not operate in a vacuum. Leaders may be mindful of all the issues that come with creating different employment arrangements for members of the same group, such as coordinating work schedules and task assignments and maintaining perceptions of fairness. While an accommodating workgroup can enable the leader to grant i-deals to individual members, a nonsupportive group can stop the leader from entertaining any i-deal negotiations. Indeed, Hornung and his colleagues (2008) found that organizations used to the concept of nontraditional work arrangements such as telecommuting are more open to making i-deals. Other research has shown that managers are less likely to grant i-deals in large workgroups, possibly due to increased difficulties in coordination across group members (Hornung, Rousseau, & Glaser, 2009). Research has also shown that workgroup culture can limit the beneficial effects of i-deals (Bal, De Jong, Jansen, & Bakker, 2012). More research is needed to explore how the structural and social attributes of the workgroup shape group members' i-deals. In the following section, we explore how an important social attribute – organizational culture – can influence the relationship between leadership style and i-deals.

Leadership style and i-deals: moderating effect of organizational culture

Organizational culture is described as shared values and beliefs that affect employees' perceptions and behaviors (Schein, 2004). There are at least two reasons why organizational culture may impact the strength of the relationship between employees' perceptions of their leaders and their likelihood of seeking i-deals. First, because organizational culture influences individuals' perceptions and attitudes, it may affect the propensity to seek i-deals formed as a result of perceptions about leadership. When employees' perceptions of managers' leadership are in sync with organizational norms and expectations, it may produce a synergistic effect on employees' propensity to seek i-deals. For example, employees in organizations characterized by achievement orientation (Tziner & Falbe, 1990) may value individualized and differentiated relationship with leaders, and, therefore, positive leadership perceptions likely accrue substantial increase in i-deals. Second, organizational culture portrays goals and principles that are important to entities. Because individual goals are interlinked with and dependent on the work environment, granting and seeking of i-deals may partially depend on the organizational cultural context. Specifically, employees in organizations characterized by i-deals–friendly cultures may show a weaker relationship between perceptions of leadership and levels of i-deals. In an organization where established cultural code and value system encourages i-deals, employees are likely to achieve i-deals even without much support from the leader. Therefore, we posit that organizational culture dimensions such as respect for people, aggressiveness, and team orientation (O'Reilly, Chatman, & Caldwell, 1991) interact with employee perceptions of leadership and influence the levels of i-deals.

Respect for people

Respect for people is one of the employee-directed dimensions of the organizational cultural profile (OCP) that describes organizational norms concerning justice, tolerance, and regard for individuals (O'Reilly et al., 1991). Organizations scoring high on the respect for people dimension of OCP show greater concern for their employees by preserving their individual rights. Employees in organizations with high respect for people receive respectful treatment from others (Erdogan, Liden, & Kraimer, 2006). Because the respect for people dimension of OCP signifies the importance of individuals' rights in organizations, organizations are likely to bestow i-deals to employees irrespective of their perceptions of leadership. Furthermore, high respect for people indicates that organizations have high tolerance in individuals' work preferences (e.g., Sheridan, 1992). In an organization with high respect for people orientation, a greater number of employees is likely to seek and get i-deals regardless of the extent to which the leader is viewed as supportive. As a result, the effects of leadership style on employees' i-deals will be less pronounced in organizations with high rather than low respect for people culture.

> *Proposition 5a: The respect for people dimension of OCP will moderate the relationship between leadership style and i-deals, such that the relationship will be weaker in organizations with high (vs. low) respect for people.*

Aggressiveness

The aggressiveness dimension of the OCP describes the shared perception of the acceptable level of competitiveness at work, such that organizations high on the aggressiveness dimension value individual aggression more than communal dependability. Aggressive organizations encourage employees to achieve higher outcomes. Organizations with aggressive cultures encourage individuals to surpass others rather than forge harmonious relationships at work (O'Reilly et al., 1991). Because aggressiveness emphasizes the importance of individual initiative and individual rewards over development of close relationships with peers (Sheridan, 1992), individualized consideration from leaders, regardless of peers' discomfort, is likely to result in higher i-deals. Because aggressive organizations are result oriented, loyalty to coworkers is not a part of the organizational schema. Aggressive organizations expect their members to outperform others at work and therefore seeking i-deals likely become an end as well as means to meet other outcome goals.

> *Proposition 5b: The aggressiveness dimension of OCP will moderate the relationship between leadership style and i-deals, such that the relationship will be stronger in organizations high (vs. low) on aggressiveness.*

Team orientation

Team orientation describes shared values and norms regarding the importance of and the correct ways of relating to other team members in the organization (O'Reilly et al., 1991). Organizations scoring high on team orientation reward collaboration rather than competition among its members. Similar to the collectivistic dimension of societal culture (Hofstede, 1980), employees in team-oriented organizations may forgo individual goals and rewards for the benefits of others in the work relationship. Because team orientation concerns collaboration among coworkers, employees in team-oriented organizations are expected to cooperate and share information with each other. Individualized design of i-deals may seem antithesis to the norms of a team-oriented organization. Thus, team orientation may interact with leadership perceptions and mitigate its effect on i-deals. Even when employees may develop positive perceptions of leaders' support, the normative pressure of a team-oriented culture may force employees to not seek i-deals. Finally, in a team-oriented culture if any i-deals are made, they might be attributed to the team's rather than the leader's support.

> *Proposition 5c: The team orientation dimension of OCP will moderate the relationship between leadership perceptions and i-deals, such that the relationship will be weaker in organizations high (vs. low) on team orientation.*

Consequences of i-deals: effects of differentiation

I-deals have the ability to provide employees with their desired work schedules, work locations, job responsibilities, and career development opportunities (Rousseau, 2005). Because i-deals fulfill employees' unique needs, they are likely to create obligations towards the grantor (e.g., leader and organization) and the enablers (coworkers) of the deal, which can be discharged through positive attitudes and behaviors designed to aid all of those parties (Greenberg et al., 2004). Empirical research has shown several benefits of i-deals for the receiving employee, such as enhanced perceptions of job autonomy and job satisfaction (Hornung, Rousseau, Glaser, Angerer, & Weigl, 2010; Rosen et al., 2013). I-deals benefit the organization through enhancements in favorable employee attitudes, such as affective organizational commitment and perceived organizational support (Liu, Lee, Hui, Kwan, & Wu, 2013) and positive employee behaviors, such as working unpaid overtime hours (Hornung et al., 2008) and engaging in citizenship behaviors towards coworkers, managers, and the organization itself (Anand et al., 2010). However, research in this stream has so far been limited to the individual employee's level. An exploration of i-deals across various levels of analysis, such as individual, workgroup, and organization, can further our understanding of this phenomenon. There is some evidence that the workgroup context sets boundaries to the effects of i-deals. For example, Hornung and colleagues (2008) found a positive association between developmental i-deals but not flexibility i-deals and organizational commitment, probably because the organization was widely distributing the flexibility i-deals which created a normative perception for those deals and reduced the value ascribed to them. The evaluation of i-deals and subsequent reciprocity as a function of the organizational context is an issue that needs further exploration by i-deal researchers.

I-deals differentiation and outcomes for the individual member

The individualized nature of i-deals creates heterogeneity in the workgroup, which increases the possibility of social comparison between members (Ho, 2005). The value of one's i-deal may be based on comparison with other group members' deals. Workgroups are likely to vary in the extent of i-deals given to members. Some groups may have large within-group variability as indicated by few i-deals, whereas some others may have low variability as indicated by a somewhat uniform distribution of i-deals among group members. The within-group social comparison–driven evaluations of i-deals may also be influenced by between-group differences in i-deal variability. In a group with high i-deals variability, a special deal can symbolize the recipient's relative standing in the group. Social comparison between group members is more likely to enhance the perceived value of the deal and resulting obligations to the sources of the deal in this context, as compared to a group with low variability. The relationship between i-deals and subsequent attitudes and behaviors is therefore likely to become stronger when there is large variability in i-deals within workgroups. This argument is consistent with research on LMX differentiation, a phenomenon conceptually similar to i-deals in that both create within-group differences, which has shown that the within-group social comparison–driven positive relationship between one's relative LMX and benevolent attitudes toward the organization is stronger in groups with high variability in LMX (Henderson et al., 2008).

I-deals present a sensitive balance to the organization. It is possible that in a group with too many negotiated deals (i.e., low differentiation), employees start believing that they need to bargain for everything (Rousseau et al., 2006) and all exchanges are strictly transactional. High extent of i-deals in a workgroup may actually change the nature of exchanges between employees and organization from social to economic. In that case, employees are likely to evaluate their i-deals on a quid-pro-quo basis and not perceive any obligations that result from a social exchange. The deals may be perceived as commonplace, possibly something that the organization should have provided without any negotiation, and thus not likely to have much influence on deal recipients' attitudes and behaviors.

> *Proposition 6: I-deals differentiation will moderate the relationship between i-deals and individual employee's outcomes such as career satisfaction and performance, such that the relationship between i-deals and outcomes will be stronger in groups with high (vs. low) i-deals differentiation.*

I-deals differentiation and outcomes for the workgroup

Drawing a parallel to LMX research, it is expected that i-deals account for outcomes at multiple levels of analysis (Schriesheim et al., 2001). So, we ponder over two questions: Does i-deals differentiation influence outcomes for the team? Does i-deals differentiation work in the same way at meso and group levels? Multi-level research maintains that while a vast majority of variables are isomorphic across levels of analysis, some variables do exhibit discontinuity or behave differently at different levels of analysis (House, Rousseau, & Thomas-Hunt, 1995). Thus it is possible for i-deals differentiation to augment the individual employee's outcomes as discussed earlier, but take away from group-level outcomes. This argument is in line with multi-level research that distinguishes the effects of leadership at the group level from those at the individual level (e.g., Chen & Bliese, 2002). Exploring the outcomes of i-deals for the individual employee without thinking of the entire team may bring undesired consequences to the organization. Therefore we next explore the relationship between i-deals differentiation and team-level outcomes. We use team potency – an outcome of particular relevance to OB/HR research – as an exemplar.

The concept of team potency derives from the concept of self-efficacy, which has been defined as an individual's belief in his/her ability to successfully complete a particular task (Bandura, 1986). At the group level, potency refers to members' shared beliefs in the group's ability to be effective (Guzzo, Yost, Campbell, & Shea, 1993). Team potency beliefs motivate positive attitudes and behaviors in the workgroup. High-potency groups are confident in their capabilities to succeed across a variety of tasks. These groups treat challenging situations as opportunities, tend to quickly bounce back from their failures, and perform better than groups with low-potency beliefs (Gully, Incalcaterra, Joshi, & Beaubien, 2002). In today's complex and uncertainty-ridden knowledge-based jobs, team potency is a particularly desirable trait. According to Bandura (1986), an individual's self-efficacy beliefs grow as one goes through learning experiences and gains new knowledge and skills. When a person is able to get desired learning and career development opportunities (i.e., developmental i-deals), she is likely to feel more in control of her destiny in the workplace and competent to achieve her job-related goals. Low differentiation of i-deals indicates a group setting in which most members are able to get learning opportunities customized to further their careers in their chosen directions. The "enactive mastery" innate to i-deals enhances members' sense of empowerment and confidence in their group's ability to succeed in any given tasks. This argument is consistent with past research, which has established links between individual members' skills and perceptions of team efficacy (Tasa, Taggar, & Seijts, 2007).

High i-deals differentiation indicates a workgroup where few members are able to negotiate coveted developmental opportunities, which may create perceptions of favoritism. In contrast, workgroups with low differentiation indicate equal treatment for members, and thus increase the possibility of harmony and cooperation amongst the group members, which is further likely to enhance team potency beliefs. Finally, low differentiation for i-deals signifies a supportive environment whereby the organization, typically represented by the leader, cares for the employees' personal development. This setting is likely to be laden with mutual respect and affect, similar to a setting with high overall level of LMX, which has been shown to be associated with high team potency (Boies & Howell, 2006).

> *Proposition 7: I-deals differentiation will be negatively related to workgroup outcomes such as team potency.*

Conclusion

Our review of extant research on i-deals has revealed a strong interest in this area among both management scholars and practitioners. Considerable attention has been devoted to understanding the drivers of i-deals for the individual employee. Research has also explored the many benefits of i-deals for the individual recipient and the granting organization. However, this research still needs to develop an understanding of how i-deals function in the context of the workgroup. We strongly encourage scholars to explore various attributes of the workgroup context to further develop i-deals theory. Specifically, there continues to be a need for research that enhances our understanding of 1) the way in which various attributes of workgroup leadership influence negotiation, implementation, and results of individual member's i-deals, 2) how workgroup culture sets boundaries to these relationships, and 3) how the differences created by i-deals influence the entire workgroup.

Note

1 Smriti Anand, Illinois Institute of Technology, USA; Prajya Vidyarthi, University of Texas at El Paso, USA.

References

Anand, S., Vidyarthi, P.R., Liden, R.C., & Rousseau, D.M. (2010). Good citizens in poor-quality relationships: Idiosyncratic deals as a substitute for relationship quality. *Academy of Management Journal, 53*, 970–988.

Bal, P.M., De Jong, S.B., Jansen, P.G., & Bakker, A.B. (2012). Motivating employees to work beyond retirement: A multi-level study of the role of i-deals and unit climate. *Journal of Management Studies, 49*(2), 306–331.

Bandura, A. (1986). *Social foundations of thought and action: A social cognitive theory*. Englewood Cliffs, NJ: Prentice Hall.

Bies, R.J., & Moag, J.F. (1986). Interactional justice: Communication criteria of fairness. In R.J. Lewicki, B.H. Sheppard, & M.H. Bazerman (Eds.), *Research on negotiations in organizations* (Vol. 1, pp. 43–55). Greenwich, CT: JAI Press.

Boies, K., & Howell, J.M. (2006). Leader-member exchange in teams: An examination of the interaction between relationship differentiation and mean LMX in explaining team-level outcomes. *Leadership Quarterly, 17*, 246–257.

Cappelli, P. (2000). A market-driven approach to retaining talent. *Harvard Business Review, 78*, 103–111.

Chen, G., & Bliese, P. (2002). The role of different levels of leadership in predicting self- and collective efficacy: Evidence for discontinuity. *Journal of Applied Psychology, 87*, 549–556.

Colquitt, J.A. (2004). Does the justice of the one interact with the justice of the many? Reactions to procedural justice in teams. *Journal of Applied Psychology, 89*, 633–646.

Coyle-Shapiro, J. A-M., Shore, L.M., Taylor, M.S., & Tetrick, L.E. (Eds.). (2004). *The employment relationship: Examining psychological and contextual perspectives.* Oxford: Oxford University Press.

Erdogan, B., Liden, R.C., & Kraimer, M.L. (2006). Justice and leader–member exchange: The moderating role of organizational culture. *Academy of Management Journal, 49*, 395–406.

Festinger, L. (1954). A theory of social comparison processes. *Human Relations, 7*, 117–140.

Graen, G.B., & Uhl-Bien, M. (1995). Relationship-based approach to leadership: Development of leader–member exchange (LMX) theory of leadership over 25 years: Applying a multi-level multi-domain perspective. *Leadership Quarterly, 6*, 219–247.

Grant, A.M., & Parker, S. (2009). Redesigning work design theories: The rise of relational and proactive perspectives. *Academy of Management Annals, 3*, 317–375.

Greenberg, J., Roberge, M.E., Ho, V.T., & Rousseau, D. (2004). Fairness as an "i-deal": Justice in under-the-table employment arrangements. *Research in Personnel and Human Resources Management, 22*, 1–34.

Gully, S.M., Incalcaterra, K.A., Joshi, A., & Beaubien, J.M. (2002). A meta-analysis of team-efficacy, potency, and performance: Interdependence and level of analysis as moderators of observed relationships. *Journal of Applied Psychology, 87*, 819–832.

Guzzo, R.A., Yost, P.R., Campbell, R.J., & Shea, G.P. (1993). Potency in groups: Articulating a construct. *British Journal of Social Psychology, 32*, 87–106.

Hackman, J.R., & Oldham, G.R. (1980). *Work redesign.* Reading, MA: Addison-Wesley.

Henderson, D.J., Wayne, S.J., Shore, L.M., Bommer, W.H., & Tetrick, L.E. (2008). Leader–member exchange, differentiation, and psychological contract fulfillment: A multilevel examination. *Journal of Applied Psychology, 93*, 1208–1219.

Ho, V.T. (2005). Social influence on evaluations of psychological contract fulfillment. *Academy of Management Review, 30*, 113–128.

Hofstede, G.H. (1980). *Culture consequences: International differences in work-related values.* London: Sage.

Hornung, S., Rousseau, D.M., & Glaser, J. (2008). Creating flexibility through idiosyncratic deals. *Journal of Applied Psychology, 93*, 655–664.

Hornung, S., Rousseau, D.M., & Glaser, J. (2009). Why supervisors make idiosyncratic deals: Antecedents and outcomes of i-deals from a managerial perspective. *Journal of Managerial Psychology, 24*, 738–764.

Hornung, S., Rousseau, D.M., Glaser, J., Angerer, P., & Weigl, M. (2010). Beyond top-down and bottom-up work redesign: Customizing job content through idiosyncratic deals. *Journal of Organizational Behavior, 31*, 187–215.

Hornung, S., Rousseau, D.M., Glaser, J., Angerer, P., & Weigl, M. (2011). Employee-oriented leadership and quality of working life: Mediating roles of idiosyncratic deals. *Psychological Reports, 108*(1), 59–74.

Hornung, S., Rousseau, D.M., Weigl, M., Müller, A., & Glaser, J. (2014). Redesigning work through idiosyncratic deals. *European Journal of Work and Organizational Psychology, 23*(4), 608–626.

Hooper, D.T., & Martin, R. (2008). Beyond personal leader-member exchange (LMX) quality: The effects of perceived LMX variability on employee reactions. *Leadership Quarterly, 19*, 20–30.

House, R.J., Rousseau, D.M., & Thomas-Hunt, M. (1995). The meso paradigm: A framework for the integration of micro and macro organizational behavior. In B.M. Staw & L.L. Cummings (Eds.), *Research in organizational behavior* (Vol. 17, pp. 71–114). Greenwich, CT: JAI Press.

Lai, L., Rousseau, D.M., & Chang, T.T.K. (2009). Idiosyncratic deals: Coworkers as interested third parties. *Journal of Applied Psychology, 94*, 547–556.

Lawler, E.E., III, & Finegold, D. (2000). Individualizing the organization: Past, present, and future. *Organizational Dynamics, 294*, 1–15.

Leventhal, G.S. (1980). What should be done with equity theory? New approaches to the study of fairness in social relationships. In K. Gergen, M. Greenberg, & R. Willis (Eds.), *Social exchange: Advances in theory and research* (pp. 27–55). New York: Plenum Press.

Liden, R.C., Erdogan, B., Wayne, S.J., & Sparrowe, R.T. (2006). Leader-member exchange, differentiation, and task interdependence: Implications for individual and group performance. *Journal of Organizational Behavior, 27*, 723–746.

Liden, R.C., & Graen, G. (1980). Generalizability of the vertical dyad linkage model of leadership. *Academy of Management Journal, 23*, 451–465.

Liu, J., Lee, C., Hui, C., Kwan, H.K., & Wu, L.-Z. (2013). Idiosyncratic deals and employee outcomes: The mediating roles of social exchange and self-enhancement and the moderating role of individualism. *Journal of Applied Psychology, 98*, 832–841.

Morrison, E.W., & Robinson, S.L. (1997). When employees feel betrayed: A model of how psychological contract violation develops. *Academy of Management Review, 22*, 226–256.

O'Reilly, C.A., Chatman, J.A., & Caldwell, D.F. (1991). People and organizational culture: A profile comparison approach to assessing person-organization fit. *Academy of Management Journal, 34*, 487–516.

Rosen, C.C., Slater, D., Chang, C., & Johnson, R.E. (2013). Let's make a deal: Development and validation of the ex-post i-deals scale. *Journal of Management, 39*, 709–742.

Rousseau, D.M. (2001). Idiosyncratic deals: Flexibility versus fairness? *Organizational Dynamics, 29*, 260–271.

Rousseau, D.M. (2005). *I-deals: Idiosyncratic deals employees bargain for themselves*. New York: M.E. Sharpe.

Rousseau, D.M., Ho, V.T., & Greenberg, J. (2006). I-deals: Idiosyncratic terms in employment relationships. *Academy of Management Review, 31*, 977–994.

Schein, E.H. (2004). *Organizational culture and leadership*. San Francisco, CA: Jossey-Bass.

Schriesheim, C.A., Castro, S.L., Zhou, X., & Yammarino, F.J. (2001). The folly of theorizing "A" but testing "B": A selective level-of-analysis review of the field and a detailed leader–member exchange illustration. *Leadership Quarterly, 12*, 515–551.

Sheridan, J. (1992). Organizational culture and employee retention. *Academy of Management Journal, 35*, 1036–1056

Simons, T., & Roberson, Q. (2003). Why managers should care about fairness: The effects of aggregate justice perceptions on organizational outcomes. *Journal of Applied Psychology, 88*, 432–443.

Sy, T., Côté, S., & Saavedra, R. (2005). The contagious leader: Impact of the leader's mood on the mood of group members, group affective tone, and group processes. *Journal of Applied Psychology, 90*, 295–305.

Tasa, K., Taggar, S., & Seijts, G.H. (2007). The development of collective efficacy in teams: A multilevel and longitudinal perspective. *Journal of Applied Psychology, 92,* 17–27.

Tziner, A., & Falbe, C.M. (1990). Actual and preferred climates of achievement orientation and their congruency: An investigation of their relationships to work attitudes and performance in two occupational strata. *Journal of Organizational Behavior, 11,* 159–167.

Wrzesniewski, A., & Dutton, J.E. (2001). Crafting a job: Revisioning employees as active crafters of their work. *Academy of Management Review, 26,* 179–201.

8
EQUITY VERSUS NEED

How do coworkers judge the distributive fairness of i-deals?

Elise Marescaux and Sophie De Winne[1]

Introduction

Rousseau's (2005) book on i-deals has inspired researchers to study idiosyncratic deals or "i-deals" as a means of introducing differentiation in working conditions. I-deals are personalized employment arrangements negotiated between employee and employer and are characterized by four features (Rousseau, 2005): (1) the arrangement applies to one employee only (i.e., the i-dealer); (2) i-deals result from a negotiation between i-dealer and employer; (3) the arrangement can vary from a single feature to an entire idiosyncratic employment relationship; and (4) the i-deal creates a win–win situation for both employee (i.e., the arrangement itself) and employer (i.e., the potential of i-deals to attract, motivate, and retain valuable employees).

    This rising interest in i-deals results from a competitive labor market coupled with a workforce that has increasingly diverse needs and preferences and wants to be treated as individuals (Greenberg, Roberge, Ho, & Rousseau, 2004; Marescaux, De Winne, & Sels, 2013a; Rousseau, 2005). Offering individualized employment conditions thus becomes necessary to attract, motivate, and retain employees. Previous empirical work has mainly concentrated on the impact of i-deals on i-dealers, showing that they generate affective organizational commitment, organizational citizenship behavior, and work engagement (Anand, Vidyarthi, Liden, & Rousseau, 2010; Hornung, Rousseau, Glaser, Angerer, & Weigl, 2010; Ng & Feldman, 2010). However, from an organizational perspective, it is crucial to study coworker reactions as well. Firstly, coworkers can choose to refrain from actively supporting the i-deal, which can be required for an i-deal to be effective (e.g., in the case of task switches). Secondly, negative reactions can counter the positive impact of the i-deal such that it is reduced, neutralized, or even outbalanced (Rousseau, 2005). Finally, if negative reactions are directed towards the i-dealer (e.g., hostility), this can affect the i-dealer's attitudes, behavior, and performance negatively, thus additionally thwarting the ideal's benefits (Chiaburu & Harrison, 2008). As such, i-deals are suggested to be most successful when they create a win–win situation benefiting both i-dealer and employer, without generating negative coworker reactions (Rousseau, 2005).

A crucial driver of coworker reactions is believed to be organizational justice, because i-deals introduce exceptions to the rule which can give rise to questions of fairness (Lai, Rousseau, & Chang, 2009). A principal role can be assigned to distributive justice, as people will mainly consider the fairness of procedures and interactions when a decision outcome is seen as distributively unfair (Colella, Paetzold, & Belliveau, 2004). Accordingly, distributive justice judgments have shown to give rise to a wide range of employee reactions, such as higher work performance and organizational citizenship behavior and less counterproductive work behavior and conflict (Cohen-Charash & Spector, 2001). In addition, in the specific context of i-deals, Marescaux, De Winne, and Sels (2013b) showed that i-deals that are perceived as distributively unjust can increase the odds that coworkers will exhibit counterproductive behavior (e.g., withholding effort). Given the importance of coworkers' distributive justice perceptions, insights are needed into how these perceptions are formed. From the distributive justice literature, we learn that people can judge the fairness of an outcome differently depending on the distributive rule they use. In this study, we specifically focus on two rules: equity and need. We study equity because it is considered the predominant rule in organizations (Morand & Merriman, 2012) and need because i-deals aim to address the increasing individual needs of the workforce (Rousseau, 2005). As such, a first objective of this study is to examine whether coworkers judge the distributive fairness of i-deals based on equity, need, or a combination of both.

Secondly, distributive justice theory suggests that the way people judge the fairness of allocation outcomes depends on the type of resource involved in the allocation. More specifically, allocations that involve universal (i.e., valued by all employees) and scarce (i.e., part of a fixed pie) resources (e.g., money) are more likely to be judged using the equity rule as employees try to protect the scarce resource and their share of it (Leventhal, Karuza, & Fry, 1980). In contrast, allocations involving more particularistic and relatively less scarce resources (e.g., flexibility and developmental opportunities) differ relatively more in the value that employees derive from them, reducing the odds that they use the equity rule to assess their distributive fairness. In addition, these allocations are relatively more aimed at increasing employee well-being and/or personal development, increasing the use of the need rule to assess distributive fairness (Leventhal et al., 1980). Therefore, a second objective of this study is to study whether the type of i-deal determines how coworkers will assess its distributive justice, distinguishing between i-deals involving universal and scarce resources (i.e., financial i-deals) and i-deals involving particularistic and less scarce resources (i.e., flexibility and job content i-deals).

Finally, the literature on distributive justice suggests that perceptions of distributive justice can vary across people (Cohen-Charash & Spector, 2001). An important individual factor in this regard is gender. Research has shown that when asked to allocate rewards between themselves and others, women divide these rewards differently than men (Major & Adams, 1983). This is argued to result from different views on distributive justice. Whereas women prefer an allocation that maintains welfare and social relationships, men tend to prefer an equitable allocation focusing on task performance and maximizing their own gain (Tata, 2000). However, to our knowledge, no attempts have been made to investigate whether this also implies that women and men use different rules to judge the fairness of a certain allocation (e.g., an i-deal) in their organization. As such, a final objective of this study is to establish whether the coworker's gender determines how the distributive fairness of an i-deal is judged.

We aim to advance the literature on i-deals in several ways. We abandon the nearly exclusive focus on the impact of i-deals on i-dealers by focusing on coworkers' distributive judgments of an i-deal. Doing so, we unravel how i-deals can create a win–win situation for both the organization and the i-dealer without causing perceptions of outcome unfairness and subsequent negative coworker reactions. We specifically unravel this by exploring on which basis (need and/or equity) coworkers assess the distributive justice of an i-deal and by considering two variables that can determine this: i-deal content and coworker gender. In this way, we sort out the complexity of managing coworker reactions to i-deals by investigating how i-deals and their distributive fairness can be perceived quite differently depending on the principle used to judge them, the coworker in question, and the type of i-deal. As such, this study is also relevant for practitioners as it provides organizations with insights into how they can effectively implement and legitimize i-deals, thereby maximizing perceptions of distributive justice.

Literature review and hypotheses

Equity and need as the basis of an i-deal's distributive justice

Employees can use different rules to assess the distributive justice of a certain outcome. Traditional distributive justice literature has identified three dominant distributive justice principles: equality, equity, and need (Deutsch, 1975; Leventhal et al., 1980). The principle of equality entails that decision outcomes are considered fair insofar as all employees receive the same outcomes. Equity implies that outcomes are considered just insofar as the outputs of employees (e.g., pay, benefits) are proportional to the inputs (e.g., skills, performance) across employees (Adams, 1965). Finally, the need rule signifies that outcome allocations are considered fair insofar as they are in line with employees' needs. In this study, we focus specifically on equity and need, reflecting two principles that coworkers can use to assess the distributive justice of i-deals. We choose to drop equality because the use of this principle by coworkers would automatically entail perceptions of distributive injustice as by definition i-deals create nonequality in the workplace. The principles of equity and need, on the other hand, allow fair outcome differentiation between employees, insofar as the differences are based on equity or need.

Firstly, equity is considered the predominant rule used by (employees in) organizations (Morand & Merriman, 2012). Equity theory (Adams, 1965) suggests that employees compare their work inputs (e.g., effort, time) with their work outputs (e.g., pay, benefits) and compare this ratio with referent coworkers to assess distributive justice (Carrell & Dittrich, 1978). More specifically, if employees perceive an imbalance between their inputs and outputs in comparison to others, they will perceive distributive unfairness. Applying equity to the context of i-deals implies that an i-deal would be considered distributively unfair when it distorts the input/output balance of the i-dealer in comparison to the coworker. For example, an i-deal can imply that the i-dealer receives more rewards (e.g., money, status, benefits) than the coworker in exchange for the same inputs or that the i-dealer is allowed to deliver less input (e.g., through a workload reduction) for the same output. In contrast, the i-deal would be considered distributively fair insofar as the i-deal maintains or restores the balance (e.g., when the i-deal is a reward for exceptional performance).

Secondly, despite the prevalence of equity in organizational research, some, albeit fairly few, scholars have also stressed the importance of employee needs as a driver of outcome distributions (e.g., Colella, 2001; Day, Holladay, Johnson, & Barron, 2014). Especially in a context of i-deals, the need rule could be highly relevant as i-deals aim to address the increasingly diverse individual needs and preferences of the workforce (Rousseau, 2005). This implies that an i-deal would be considered distributively fair by coworkers when it is perceived to address a specific individual need of the i-dealer. For example, flexibility i-deals can be granted to employees in response to a high need for work–life balance. In contrast, an i-deal would be judged distributively unfair when coworkers do not believe that the i-dealer has a specific need for it.

The above suggests that the distributive fairness of i-deals could be judged on an equity or need basis. However, this does not imply that these distributive justice principles are mutually exclusive. Leventhal et al. (1980) argued that employees can prefer the use of several principles to allocate outcomes in the workplace, attaching equal importance to them or attaching more importance to one or the other (e.g., favoring equity over need). The degree to which employees favor one principle over the other is however argued to be situation- and person-dependent (Leventhal et al., 1980), on which we will elaborate further below when we consider the role of i-deal content and coworker gender. In general, however, this suggests that both perceived equity and perceived need can influence coworkers' judgment of distributive justice in a positive manner, leading to the following first set of hypotheses:

Hypothesis 1a. The more a coworker perceives an i-deal to be equitably allocated, the higher his or her perceptions of the i-deal's distributive justice.

Hypothesis 1b. The more a coworker perceives an i-deal to be allocated based on the i-dealer's need, the higher his or her perceptions of the i-deal's distributive justice.

The i-deal's content

Rosen, Slater, Chang, and Johnson (2013) argued and found that i-deals can take different forms: i-deals concerning (1) job content, (2) financial incentives, (3) flexibility in work schedule, and (4) flexibility in work location. The first type of i-deals consists of arrangements concerning how many and which duties employees need to perform in their job (e.g., negotiating more personally challenging or interesting assignments or a [temporary] workload reduction). Financial i-deals concern financial arrangements that differ from the standard rewards allocated to employees (e.g., additional bonuses or benefits). The final two i-deals concern the increase of flexibility, both in terms of work schedules and work location.

These i-deals differ in the degree to which the resources they distribute are universal (vs. particularistic) and scarce. Universal resources are resources that have common meaning and value across employees, whereas particularistic resources can be valued differently by employees (Foa & Foa, 1974; Rousseau, Ho, & Greenberg, 2006). Money is a typical universal resource in the sense that its value to employees is relatively universal and independent of who allocates the resource. In addition, it is generally a scarce resource as organizations only have a limited amount of money to distribute across their employees. Due to its universal value and scarcity, the use of the equity rule becomes relatively more likely than the need rule, in an effort to protect the scarce resource and one's share of it (Leventhal et al., 1980). In addition, money is a typical resource that is perceived to be distributed by organizations to increase employee performance (e.g., pay-for-performance schemes). This increases the odds that employees will apply the equity rule, taking performance into account (Leventhal et al., 1980). In sum, this would suggest that i-deals that concern money (i.e., financial i-deals) are relatively more prone to equity evaluations than need evaluations.

In contrast, the other two types of i-deals (i.e. flexibility and job content) are concerned with more particularistic resources, as employees can differ relatively more in the value they derive from flexibility and job content. This implies that employees will also differ relatively more in the degree to which they value these types of i-deals, reducing the odds that they will adopt the equity rule in an effort to protect the resources distributed through these i-deals and their share of it (Leventhal et al., 1980). Moreover, both i-deals are relatively more aimed at increasing employee well-being (e.g., increasing work–life balance through flexibility) or personal development (e.g., more challenging job assignments). This increases the relative importance that employees will attach to the need rule compared to the equity rule (Leventhal et al., 1980). As such, we hypothesize the following:

> **Hypothesis 2a.** For i-deals concerning financial incentives, the degree to which a coworker perceives the allocation of the i-deal to be equitable will have a larger impact on his/her perception of the i-deal's distributive justice than the degree to which he/she perceives it to be allocated based on the i-dealer's need.

> **Hypothesis 2b.** For i-deals concerning job content and flexibility, the degree to which a coworker perceives the allocation of the i-deal to be based on the i-dealer's need will have a larger impact on his/her perception of the i-deal's distributive justice than the degree to which he/she perceives the i-deal to be equitably allocated.

The coworker's gender

Ample research has shown that men and women allocate rewards differently among themselves and others (Major & Adams, 1983; Tata, 2000). More specifically, traditional justice research has consistently found that, when asked to divide a reward between themselves and others, men tend to take equity into greater account than do women (Major & Adams, 1983). Generally, it is suggested that this occurs because men and women differ in their orientations and goals and subsequently their take on distributive justice. This can be deduced from social role theory (Eagly, 1987), which suggests that typical gender roles include women to be more socially oriented, focusing on the welfare of others (Eckel & Grossman, 1998; Major & Adams, 1983; Tata, 2000). This tendency towards social responsibility or concern for others can subsequently increase the likelihood that the need rule will be used to assess distributive justice (Colella, 2001; Leventhal, 1976). Men on the other hand are more individually oriented, competitive, and focused on tasks and maximizing their own gain (Major & Adams, 1983; Tata, 2000). This implies that men may focus more on comparing their own inputs and outputs in the job with others to ensure that they maximize their own outputs (Major, Bylsma, & Cozzarelli, 1989). As a consequence, they will focus relatively more on equity than need to assess distributive justice (Brockner & Adsit, 1986). Translated to the context of i-deals, this would imply that women have a relatively higher tendency to assess the distributive justice of an i-deal based on perceived need than equity, whereas men would attach relatively more importance to perceived equity than need. This results in the following hypothesis:

> **Hypothesis 3a.** Among female coworkers, the degree to which they perceive the i-deal to be allocated based on the i-dealer's need will have a stronger impact on their perceptions of distributive justice than the degree to which they perceive the i-deal to be equitably allocated.

> **Hypothesis 3b.** Among male coworkers, the degree to which they perceive the i-deal to be equitably allocated will have a stronger impact on their perceptions of distributive justice than the degree to which they perceive the i-deal to be allocated based on the i-dealer's need.

Methodology

Procedure and sample

We made use of a questionnaire which was part of a biennial nationwide web survey concerning pay and employment conditions. During May and June 2008, participants were invited to fill in the survey through advertisements in two Belgian job magazines, their website, and radio commercials. We first provided respondents with a description of the concept "i-deals" in line with Rousseau's (2005) definition, after which we asked them whether they could recall a recent i-deal in their work environment, negotiated by one of their colleagues. Of 24,575 respondents, 7,616 (31%) answered positively. To reduce the time frame and increase the reliability of answers, we removed respondents of which the i-deal dated back to more than a year ago (1,806 respondents). In addition, we removed incomplete records, resulting in a final sample of 5,521 respondents – of which 55.6% was male and the average age was 35.33 years ($SD = 9.00$). The average seniority was 6.97 years ($SD = 7.63$). Respondents worked in diverse functional domains, of which the largest are operational departments (17.8%), administration/central services (15.1%), sales (13.0%), ICT/internet services (8.9%), and technical support (8.7%). Finally, 89.2% worked full time.

Measures

Distributive justice measurements typically involve statements referring to the fairness of a certain decision outcome (e.g., "my level of pay is fair," Niehoff & Moorman, 1993). Therefore, we used three items to tap the degree to which coworkers considered the allocation of the i-deal itself to be fair (e.g., "I thought it was fair that my colleague got this arrangement," $\alpha = .96$). *Perceived equity* measures traditionally refer to the balance between one's own inputs and outputs (e.g., Leventhal, 1976). As in this study, we wanted to capture the perceived equity of an arrangement from a third-party (i.e., the coworker) perspective. We therefore developed three items referring to the balance between the i-dealer's inputs and outputs (e.g., "the arrangement created an imbalance between the performance of my colleague [i.e., the i-dealer] and what my colleague received in return from my employer," reverse coded; $\alpha = .64$). *Perceived need* refers to the degree that the i-deal was needed or warranted. As such, this was measured using three items referring to the degree to which the i-dealer had a specific need for the i-deal (e.g., "My colleague did not really need that arrangement," reverse coded; $\alpha = .88$). All items were rated on a scale from 1 (totally disagree) to 7 (totally agree).

Gender and i-deal content. Respondents were asked to report their own gender (male or female) and the content of the i-deal. Following the work of Rosen et al. (2013), we distinguished between different types of i-deals: i-deals concerning flexibility (e.g., in working hours, location, and vacation), job content (e.g., type of tasks and workload), and financial incentives (e.g., pay, benefits, and work equipment). Since, in theory, an i-deal can be a combination of several types of arrangements, we allowed respondents to check multiple responses. This proved to be highly relevant, as 42% of the respondents indicated that one i-deal was a combination of multiple types.

Control variables. We measured several control variables which could confound the relationships that are of interest to this study and affect perceptions of distributive justice: age, functional level, tenure, and a dummy variable indicating whether the respondent him- or herself has negotiated one or more i-deals with their employer (Cohen-Charash & Spector, 2001; Marescaux et al., 2013b). In addition, we controlled for i-deal content as well as coworker gender in the analyses of the hypotheses in which these variables were not the main variable of interest.

Results

Factor analyses

We first performed a CFA on all multi-item measures (perceived distributive justice, equity, and need). The model was assessed using several goodness-of-fit indices: SRMR ($\leq .10$), RMSEA ($\leq .08$), CFI ($\geq .90$), and TLI ($\geq .90$) (Bentler, 1990; Byrne, 2001). A satisfactory fit was attained: SRMR (.03), RMSEA (.07), CFI (.98), and TLI (.97). All observed variables had significant loadings on the intended latent variables ranging from .43 to .96. In addition, to test whether our constructs were significantly different, we estimated several alternative models. First, we tested two-factor models in which the items of two of the three factors loaded onto one factor. This resulted in three two-factor models which were all considerably worse than the three-factor model ($\Delta\chi^2$ ranging from 455.24 to 3389.63; $p < .001$). Second, a one-factor model also showed to be a worse fit to the data than the three-factor model ($\Delta\chi^2 = 3660.40$; $p < .001$). Hence, we can conclude that the three constructs are sufficiently distinct.

Descriptive statistics

Table 8.1 provides descriptive statistics on the variables of interest. We used phi coefficients, point biserial correlations, and Pearson correlations because our data consisted of both dichotomous and continuous variables. In line with our hypotheses, both perceived equity ($r(5519) = .65, p < .001$) and perceived need ($r(5519) = .71, p < .001$) were found to correlate positively with distributive justice.

TABLE 8.1 Descriptive Statistics and Correlations

	Mean	SD	1	2	3	4	5	6	7
1. Gender coworker (1 = male)	0.56	0.50	1						
2. Flexibility	0.62	0.49	−.09***	1	1	1			
3. Job content	0.33	0.47	.02	.07***	−.14***				
4. Financial	0.55	0.50	.08***	−.47***					
5. Perceived equity	3.59	1.42	.05***	.01	−.10***	−.05**	1		
6. Perceived need	4.03	1.73	.01	.24***	−.00	−.29***	.55***	1	
7. Perceived distributive justice	4.10	1.95	.10***	.10***	−.04**	−.17***	.65***	.71***	1

Note: ** $p < .01$; *** $p < .001$

Regression analyses

Several regression analyses were performed in MPLUS (Table 8.2). In a first regression, both perceived equity (β = .36; p < .001) and perceived need (β = .50; p < .001) were found to affect perceived distributive justice positively, supporting both Hypotheses 1a and 1b. Moreover, a Wald chi-square test of parameter equalities showed that perceived need had a significantly larger impact than perceived equity (F = 10.59; p < .001) (Muthén & Muthén, 2010). A second multi-group regression estimated the impact of perceived need and equity for the three types of i-deals separately. In support of Hypothesis 2a, the results show that for financial i-deals, perceived equity plays a significantly larger role than perceived need (F = 22.54; p < .001). Hypothesis 2b is equally supported as for i-deals concerning job content and flexibility; perceived equity has a significantly smaller impact on perceptions of distributive justice than perceived need (respectively F = 23.48; p < .001 and F = 101.56; p < .001). A final multi-group regression estimated the impact of perceived need and equity for men and women separately. This showed that perceived need has a larger impact than perceived equity for women (F = 13.52; p < .001), whereas both have an equal impact for men (F = 1.65; p = .20). As such, Hypothesis 3a is fully supported, whereas Hypothesis 3b is only partially supported.

In sum, the results firstly suggest that both the perceived equity of and need for an i-deal influence coworker perceptions of distributive justice in a positive manner, with perceived need outweighing the impact of perceived equity. Secondly, for i-deals concerning flexibility and job content, perceived need outweighs perceived equity, while the reverse is found for financial i-deals. Finally, perceived need has a larger impact than perceived equity for women, whereas both equally affect perceptions of outcome fairness for men.

Discussion

This study sought to contribute to the i-deals literature by examining how coworkers assess the distributive justice of an i-deal. We focused first on equity, which is considered the predominant principle of distributive justice used by (employees in) organizations (Morand & Merriman, 2012). Accordingly, our results suggested that coworkers who perceive an i-deal negotiated by an employee in their organization to be equitable (e.g., as a reward for exceptional performance or effort), are more likely to judge the i-deal as distributively fair. Moreover, we focused on need as a distributive justice principle, which so far has received relatively little attention in research. We found that perceived need is at least equally important as equity. Across all employees and types of i-deals, the degree to which the i-dealer was perceived to need the i-deal had a significantly stronger impact on perceptions of outcome fairness than on perceived equity. To some degree, this contradicts the classical notion of distributive justice defined as equity in organizations (Morand & Merriman, 2012). However, our results are in line with the reasoning behind i-deals, which stresses both equity and need as i-deals are a means of addressing individual needs of valuable, high-performing employees in order to attract, motivate, and retain them (Rousseau, 2005).

TABLE 8.2 Standardized Results of Regression Analyses of Distributive Justice Perceptions Regressed on the Perceived Equity of and Need for an I-Deal

	Hypothesis 1 (n = 5,521)	Hypothesis 2: i-deal content			Hypothesis 3: Gender coworker	
		Flexibility (n = 3,419)	Job Content (n = 1,824)	Financial (n = 3,049)	Women (n = 2,449)	Men (n = 3,072)
Control variables —						
Age (in years)	-.02	-.01	.01	-.02	.01	-.04★
Organizational tenure (in years)	.00	-.01	.00	.00	-.02	.01
Functional level[a]:						
- Operational staff	-.01	-.01	-.01	-.03	-.01	.00
- Professional staff	.02	.01	-.01	.01	.01	.03
- Middle management	.03★	.02	.01	.01	.01	.04
- Higher management	.03★★	.01	.01	.02	.04★★	.04★
Own i-deal (1 = yes)	.05★★★	.05★★★	.05★★	.05★★★	.05★★★	.05★★★
I-deal content[b]:						
- Flexibility	-.03★★	/	-.01	-.02	-.05★★★	-.01
- Job content	-.01	.01	/	-.01	.01	-.02
- Financial	-.03★★	-.03★	-.03★★	/	-.05★★★	-.01
Gender respondent (1 = man)	.06★★★	.07★★★	.05★★	.09★★★	/	/
Independent variables						
Perceived equity	.36★★★	.27★★★	.32★★★	.46★★★	.34★★★	.38★★★
Perceived need	.51★★★	.60★★★	.56★★★	.37★★★	.54★★★	.49★★★
Wald chi-square test of parameter equalities (equity vs need)						
Value	11.89	101.56	23.48	22.54	13.52	1.65
p-value	.00	.00	.00	.00	.00	0.20

Note: ★ $p < .05$; ★★ $p < .01$; ★★★ $p < .001$; [a] reference category: Administrative staff;
[b] categories were not mutually exclusive, such that i-deals could be a combination of several categories

The above suggests that – at least in the context of i-deals – need may be the dominant principle rather than equity to assess distributive justice in organizations. However, we did find that this finding should be nuanced as the degree to which need dominates over equity or vice versa seems to be situation- and person-dependent. Firstly, we found the dominant principle to be dependent on the specific content of the i-deal. When i-deals concern universal and scarce resources such as money and benefits, equity outweighs need when considering the fairness of such an i-deal, in an effort to protect these resources. In contrast, when i-deals entail particularistic and less scarce resources such as flexibility and job content, need outweighs equity. To some degree, this could also be explained by the attributions employees make concerning the goal of an i-deal. Whereas financial i-deals may be more easily perceived to be allocated by the employer to increase employee's performance, flexibility and job content i-deals may be perceived to be allocated to increase employee's well-being and personal development. While the first attribution increases the relative importance of equity, the second one increases the relative importance of need (Leventhal et al., 1980).

Secondly, in line with the traditional belief that female workers are socially oriented and focus on welfare (Tata, 2000), we found perceived need to be relatively more important for female coworkers than perceived equity. However, contrary to the typical stereotype of men who are focused on tasks and maximizing their own gain, men were found to equally value equity and need when they assess the distributive justice of an i-deal. This suggests that traditional gender differences in distributive justice preferences may be less prevalent and clear-cut than one would expect. This could be the result of increasing similarity in workplace values and preferences among men and women, e.g., due to increasing participation of women in the labor market (Gilbert, Burnett, Phau, & Haar, 2010; Lee & Farh, 1999). An alternative explanation is that traditional research on the differences in allocations between men and women often studies this in a context of financial resources (i.e., dividing rewards between themselves and others) (e.g., Eckel & Grossman, 1998; Major & Adams, 1983). Indeed, if we analyze the difference between men and women for financial i-deals only, we find that men attach more importance to perceived equity ($\beta = .48$, $p < .001$) than need ($\beta = .35$, $p < .001$) ($F = 20.94$, $p < .001$) to judge the distributive fairness of an i-deal. In contrast, women attach equal importance to perceived equity ($\beta = .45$, $p < .001$) and need ($\beta = .40$, $p < .001$) ($F = 3.48$, $p = .06$). For the two other types of i-deals, we find that both men and women attach more importance to perceived need than perceived equity, suggesting that the traditional assumptions of men are only prominent in the case of financial i-deals.

Practical implications

Research on coworkers' distributive judgments of i-deals has practical relevance because they can affect their behavioral reactions (e.g., counterproductive behavior), which can influence the effectiveness of i-deals (Cohen-Charash & Spector, 2001; Marescaux et al., 2013b). We found that both perceived equity and need have an impact on perceptions of distributive justice. This implies that employers who grant i-deals can benefit from allocating these i-deals on a need and/or equity basis. The latter can be achieved by granting i-deals based on inputs such as performance, tenure, or skills (Walster, Hatfield, Walster, & Berscheid, 1978). More importantly, however, the reasoning behind the i-deal allocation must be communicated in a clear and consistent manner to coworkers such that they perceive a high degree of need and equity, and subsequently distributive justice.

Yet, we did find significant differences between types of i-deals. Our results suggest that for financial i-deals, HR managers and supervisors can mainly benefit from allocating these i-deals on an equity basis, taking into account inputs such as performance, tenure, and/or skills (Walster et al., 1978). In contrast, for i-deals concerning job content and flexibility, allocation on a needs basis is the main way to assure high outcome fairness among coworkers. However, in both cases, the other distributive rule should not be ignored, as for all types of i-deals both perceived equity and need proved to affect perceptions of distributive justice among coworkers. Finally, we found significant differences based on gender. Our results suggest that for female coworkers, perceived need is of higher importance than perceived equity. This implies that it is especially important to communicate to female coworkers whether i-deals address specific needs in order to safeguard their perceptions of distributive justice.

Limitations and directions for future research

This study is not without its limitations. Firstly, because we asked respondents to recall an i-deal and report on it, respondents may have found it difficult remembering the facts accurately, which could cause a recall bias in our results. While we cannot exclude this bias entirely, we did however reduce the risk substantially by reducing the time frame to a maximum of one year. Secondly, as our study relied on self-reported data, it may be susceptible to common method bias. To address this issue, we tested both convergent and discriminant validity (Anderson & Gerbing, 1988). First, an excellent fit was obtained for the model in which all items loaded on the factor for which they are hypothesized to be an indicator (SRMR = .03; RMSEA = .07; CFI = .98; and TLI = .97). In addition, all estimated parameter coefficients were significant, which suggests that convergent validity can be concluded. Second, we estimated several models in which the correlation between a pair of factors was constrained to 1. The fits of these constrained models were significantly worse than the fit of the unconstrained model (χ^2 differences ranging from 315.47 to 3304.14; $p < .001$). In addition, a one-factor model proved to be a bad fit to the data (SRMR = .07; RMSEA = .17; CFI = .89; and TLI = .85). As such, we can also conclude discriminant validity, suggesting that common method bias has not plagued our study substantially.

Finally, this study offers some interesting avenues for research. While we considered gender and i-deal content as factors determining how coworkers assess distributive justice, other situational factors could also play a major role. For example, when coworkers feel empathy and liking towards the i-dealer, they may be more likely to assess distributive justice on a needs basis (Colella, 2001; Leventhal, 1976). Also, to explain why the content of an i-deal could influence the degree to which equity or need dominate employees perceived outcome fairness, we relied partly on the attributions that employees may make concerning i-deals. We argued that financial i-deals may be perceived as a way to enhance performance, whereas flexibility and job content i-deals could be perceived as a means to increase well-being and personal development. Future research could further explore whether this indeed explains why employees assess outcome fairness based on mainly equity or need. Finally, we focused entirely on distributive justice because perceptions of outcome unfairness can give rise to a wide range of negative reactions, such as lower work performance and organizational citizenship behavior and more counterproductive work behavior and conflict (Cohen-Charash & Spector, 2001). However, organizational justice research has also consistently found that procedural justice can buffer this negative impact (Brockner & Wiesenfeld, 1996). As is the case for distributive justice, procedural justice is judged using different rules, more specifically, consistency, correctability, accuracy, bias suppression, ethicality, and representativeness (Leventhal, 1980). Similarly, the prevalence of these rules to assess the procedural justice of i-deals could be studied in future research, especially as research has shown that the importance of these rules is situation dependent. For example, Colquitt and Jackson (2006) found that consistency is more important in team contexts than in work environments in which employees work independently.

Conclusion

This chapter aimed to increase insights into how coworkers assess the outcome fairness of an i-deal negotiated by an employee in their work environment (the i-dealer). We found that two principles of distributive justice play an important role in this regard: perceived equity and need. Coworkers who perceive an i-deal to be equitable (e.g., as a reward for exceptional performance) or needed by the i-dealer are more likely to judge the i-deal as distributively fair. In general, we found that coworkers attach more importance to the perceived need for an i-deal than its perceived equity. However, this finding is highly situation- and person-dependent. Firstly, the dominance of perceived need was found only for i-deals involving particularistic and relatively nonscarce resources (e.g., flexibility and job content). In contrast, for financial i-deals comprising of a relatively scarce and universal resource (money), perceived equity was found to be more valued than perceived need. Secondly, in line with the traditional belief in socially oriented women who are focused on welfare, perceived need was valued more highly by female coworkers than perceived equity. In contrast to the typical stereotype of men focused on maximizing their own gain, men were found to equally value both principles of distributive justice. To some degree, this suggests that gender differences in distributive justice judgments may be less prevalent and clear-cut than generally assumed.

Note

1 Elise Marescaux and Sophie De Winne, KU Leuven, Belgium.

References

Adams, J.S. (1965). Inequity in social exchange. In L. Berkowitz (Ed.), *Advances in experimental social psychology* (pp. 267–299). New York: Academic Press.

Anand, S., Vidyarthi, P.R., Liden, R.C., & Rousseau, D.M. (2010). Good citizens in poor-quality relationships: Idiosyncratic deals as a substitute for relationship quality. *Academy of Management Journal, 53*, 970–988.

Anderson, J.D., & Gerbing, D.W. (1988). Structural equation modeling in practice: A review and recommended two-step approach. *Psychological Bulletin, 103*(3), 411–423.

Bentler, P.M. (1990). Comparative fit indices in structural models. *Psychological Bulletin, 107*, 238–246.

Brockner, J., & Adsit, L. (1986). The moderating impact of sex on the equity–satisfaction relationship: A field study. *Journal of Applied Psychology, 71*, 585–590.

Brockner, J., & Wiesenfeld, B.M. (1996). An integrative framework for explaining reactions to decisions: Interactive effects of outcomes and procedures. *Psychological Bulletin, 120*(2), 189–208.

Byrne, B.M. (2001). *Structural equation modeling with Amos. Basic concepts application and programming*. Mahwah, NJ: Lawrence Erlbaum Associates.

Carrell, M.R., & Dittrich, J.E. (1978). Equity theory: The recent literature, methodological considerations and new directions. *Academy of Management Review, 3*(2), 202–210.

Chiaburu, D.S., & Harrison, D.A. (2008). Do peers make the place? Conceptual synthesis and meta-analysis of coworker effects on perceptions, attitudes, OCBs and performance. *Journal of Applied Psychology, 93*, 1082–1103.

Cohen-Charash, Y., & Spector, P.E. (2001). The role of justice in organizations: A meta-analysis. *Organizational Behavior and Human Decision Processes, 86*, 278–321.

Colella, A. (2001). Coworker distributive fairness judgments of the workplace accommodations of employees with disabilities. *Academy of Management Review, 26*, 100–116.

Colella, A., Paetzold, R.L., & Belliveau, M.A. (2004). Factors affecting co-worker's procedural justice inferences of the workplace accommodations of employees with disabilities. *Personnel Psychology, 57*, 1–23.

Colquitt, J.A., & Jackson, C.L. (2006) Justice in teams: The context sensitivity of justice rules across individual and team contexts. *Journal of Applied Social Psychology, 36*(4), 868–899.

Day, J., Holladay, C.L., Johnson, S.K., & Barron, L.G. (2014). Organizational rewards: Considering employee need in allocation. *Personnel Review, 43*(1), 74–95.

Deutsch, M. (1975). Equity, equality, and need: What determines which value will be used as the basis of distributive justice? *Journal of Social Issues, 31*(3), 137–149.

Eagly, A.H. (1987). *Sex differences in social behavior: A social-role interpretation*. Hillsdale, NJ: Lawrence Erlbaum Associates.

Eckel, C.C., & Grossman, P.J. (1998). Are women less selfish than men? Evidence from dictator experiments. *Economic Journal, 108*, 726–735.

Foa, U.G., & Foa, E.B. (1974). *Societal structures of the mind*. Oxford: Charles C. Thomas.

Gilbert, G.R., Burnett, M.F., Phau, I., & Haar, J. (2010). Does gender matter? A review of work-related gender commonalities. *Gender in Management: An International Journal, 25*(8), 676–699.

Greenberg, J., Roberge, M., Ho, V.T., & Rousseau, D.M. (2004). Fairness in idiosyncratic work arrangements: Justice as an i-deal. In J.J. Martocchio & G.R. Ferris (Eds.), *Research in personnel and human resource management* (Vol. 23, pp. 1–34). Amsterdam: Elsevier.

Hornung, S., Rousseau, D.M., Glaser, J., Angerer, P., & Weigl, M. (2010). Beyond top-down and bottom-up work redesign: Customizing job content through idiosyncratic deals. *Journal of Organizational Behavior, 31*, 187–215.

Lai, L., Rousseau, D.M., & Chang, K.T.T. (2009). Idiosyncratic deals: Coworkers as interested third parties. *Journal of Applied Psychology, 94*, 547–556.

Lee, C., & Farh, J.L. (1999). The effects of gender in organizational justice perception. *Journal of Organizational Behavior, 20*, 133–143.

Leventhal, G.S. (1976). The distribution of rewards and resources in groups and organizations. In L. Berkowitz & E. Walster (Eds.), *Advances in experimental social psychology* (Vol. 9, pp. 91–131). New York: Academic Press.

Leventhal, G.S. (1980). What should be done with equity theory? New approaches to the study of fairness in social relationships. In K.J. Gergen, M.S. Greenberg, & R.H. Willis (Eds.), *Social exchange: Advances in theory and research* (pp. 27–55). New York: Plenum.

Leventhal, G.S., Karuza, J., & Fry, W.R. (1980). Beyond fairness: A theory of allocation preferences. In G. Mikula (Ed.), *Justice and social interaction* (pp. 167–218). Bern: Hans Huber.

Major, B., & Adams, J.B. (1983). Role of gender, interpersonal orientation, and self-presentation in distributive-justice behavior. *Journal of Personality and Social Psychology, 45*, 598–608.

Major, B., Bylsma, W.H., & Cozzarelli, C. (1989). Gender differences in distributive justice preferences: The impact of domain. *Sex Roles, 21*(7/8), 487–497.

Marescaux, E., De Winne, S., & Sels, L. (2013a). HR practices and HRM outcomes: The role of basic need satisfaction. *Personnel Review, 42*, 4–27.

Marescaux, E., De Winne, S., & Sels, L. (2013b, August). *Co-worker reactions to i-deals: A distributive justice perspective*. Paper presented at the Annual Academy of Management Meeting, Orlando (Florida).

Morand, D.A., & Merriman, K.K. (2012). "Equality theory" as a counterbalance to equity theory in human resource management. *Journal of Business Ethics, 111*, 133–144.

Muthén, L.K., & Muthén, B.O. (2010). *MPLUS user's guide. Sixth Edition*. Los Angeles, CA: Muthén & Muthén.

Ng, T.W.H., & Feldman, D.C. (2010). Idiosyncratic deals and organizational commitment. *Journal of Vocational Behavior, 76*, 419–427.

Niehoff, B.P., & Moorman, R.H. (1993). Justice as a mediator of the relationship between methods of monitoring and organizational citizenship behaviour. *Academy of Management Journal, 36*, 527–556.

Rosen, C.C., Slater, D.J., Chang, C.D., & Johnson, R.E. (2013). Let's make a deal: Development and validation of the ex-post i-deals scale. *Journal of Management, 39*(3), 709–742.

Rousseau, D.M. (2005). *I-deals: Idiosyncratic deals employees bargain for themselves*. Armonk, NY: M. E. Sharpe.

Rousseau, D. M, Ho, V.T., & Greenberg, J. (2006). I-deals: Idiosyncratic terms in employment relationships. *Academy of Management Review, 31*(4), 977–994.

Tata, J. (2000). Influence of role and gender on the use of distributive versus procedural justice principles. *Journal of Psychology, 134*, 261–268.

Walster, E.H., Hatfield, E., Walster, G.W., & Berscheid, E. (1978). *Equity: Theory and research*. Boston, MA: Allyn & Bacon.

9
THE FUTURE OF I-DEAL RESEARCH: AN AGENDA

Matthijs Bal and Denise M. Rousseau[1]

Introduction

Idiosyncratic deals (i-deals) are common in the contemporary workplace, due to employees seeking individualized employment conditions and the decline of collective bargaining resulting in less standardized arrangements (Rousseau, 2005). I-deals as individually negotiated conditions of employment may in some organizations gradually replace HR systems and collective agreements that apply to each and every employee, with profound effects in the contemporary workplace. Even though research in i-deals continues, there is still only limited empirical knowledge as to how i-deals operate in the workplace, as well as how they influence how employee, organizations, coworkers, and other parties feel, think, and behave. This book therefore has dealt with various issues regarding the conceptualization and application of i-deals and the role of coworkers in the negotiation and effects of i-deals.

This chapter summarizes the insights of the previous chapters and discusses research areas for further advancement of understanding of i-deals in the workplace, their negotiation and impact. From these chapters, a number of emerging trends and issues can be discerned.

Trends in i-deals research

The first part of the book dealt with how i-deals arise in the first place, when employees negotiate them, and the societal conditions that support them. Moreover, this part of the book discusses the state of research in i-deals. In particular, Chapter 4 by Conway and Coyle-Shapiro summarizes the latest state of science as to what i-deals research has investigated and how it has been conceptualized and measured in empirical research. Especially with regards to conceptualization of i-deals, many questions have to be resolved in order to make any real progress in understanding the why and how of i-deals in the workplace. For instance, even though i-deals have been distinguished theoretically from favoritism and shady deals (Rousseau, 2005; Rousseau, Ho, & Greenberg, 2006), there is still little understanding as to how the individual deals employees negotiate with their employer can be perceived and treated as actual i-deals. Moreover, it is unclear whether they are the result of favoritism in the workplace, indicated for instance by the positive relationships that have been found between i-deals and LMX, or the quality of the relationship between employee and the supervisor (Rosen, Slater, Chang, & Johnson, 2013). In theory, i-deals are the product of explicit negotiations that can be legitimated in the eyes of coworkers through open communication regarding their existence and motivation (Rousseau, 2005). Coworker acceptance, discussed in the third part of the book, is part and parcel of an i-deal's legitimacy (Lai, Rousseau, & Chang, 2009) and can promote positive effects particularly for the employer who grants it in terms of trust and perceptions of supportiveness (Rousseau, 2005). However, the extent to which i-deals can be conceptualized and consequently measured, in line with the definition of Rousseau (2005), demands the translation of i-deals into an empirical setting, which poses challenges as to how to measure them. Furthermore, the definition and conceptualization of i-deals include assumptions as to the relationships of i-deals with outcomes; i-deals should be negotiated such that they benefit both employee and organization, which poses a relevant empirical question. When negotiated i-deals do not significantly correlate or predict employee motivation, performance, or another potential outcome, is it still possible to speak of an i-deal or does it disqualify a negotiated deal as a "real" i-deal? For instance, it might be the case that i-deals emerge because employees feel entitled to getting an i-deal (Naumann, Minsky, & Sturman, 2002). Hence, in line with recommendations of Conway and Coyle-Shapiro (Chapter 4), it can be argued that it should be further investigated who profits from an i-deal, including not only the employee, but also other stakeholders, such as the organization, coworkers, and family and friends outside the workplace.

Next to the discussion of how i-deals could be conceptualized and measured, the question arises in which context i-deals are negotiated. The first part of the book, Chapter 2 by Bal and Lub and Chapter 3 by Guerrero and Bentein, discusses how i-deals emerge in the particular context of a given firm and society. To begin with the latter, Guerrero and Bentein have discussed how i-deals may be negotiated in organizations in order to repair damaged relationships. Given that employees may perceive damage to their relationship with the organization (e.g., psychological contract violation), i-deals aid employers and managers to repair those relationships (Hornung, Rousseau, & Glaser, 2009). I-deals may also be granted to more marginalized employees with the possibility of putting the employment relationship on an improved footing (cf. Anand, Vidyarthi, Liden, & Rousseau, 2010). Thus, i-deals may emerge in response to relational problems, in which one party may feel that there is a need to repair or undo a situation of negativity.

Bal and Lub in their chapter discuss societal influences on i-deals and the role of larger societal trends in shaping them. In particular, an increasing dominance of individualism and neoliberalism can shift attention to what individuals can do to improve their own employment circumstances, as well as make them more responsible for their own welfare and well-being. The emergence of i-deals in a neoliberal society, they argue, creates a division between those individual employees who get i-deals, and hence redesign their employment arrangement in line with their needs and wishes, and those employees who lack such opportunities. One potential consequence is an increasing inequality in the workplace and potentially in the larger society.

The second part of the book looks at specific applications of i-deals in organizations. Chapter 5 by Nauta and van de Ven discusses how i-deals can be used in the career development of employees in organizations. Distinguishing between challenge i-deals and comfort i-deals, the authors argue that challenge i-deals can be a strong incentive for employees to develop in the organization, as well as to further shape their careers, while comfort i-deals can be used for employees facing the consequences of work–life imbalance and career stagnation or decline, and in this way maintain motivation and performance through negotiating i-deals that facilitate a more optimal fit between them and their jobs. Especially in relation to the aging workforce, i-deals can be very important for maintaining employee motivation at a higher age (Bal, De Jong, Jansen, & Bakker, 2012). Hence, when i-deals are conceptualized and used in order to facilitate employee development within their jobs and organizations and outside their organizations, they can form an important intervention for employees to promote sustainable working lives. Through negotiation of i-deals, employees can manage their careers to fit their needs and preferences for development, and at the same time, organizations can facilitate employee growth and profit from more knowledgeable employees. However, management of i-deals is crucial in the potential success of i-deals in the workplace. Nauta and van de Ven describe how a dialogue between employee and organization is necessary in order to familiarize employees in negotiation of i-deals.

Chapter 6 by Kroon, Freese, and Schalk builds upon this notion of the "management of i-deals" and discusses their relationship to strategic HRM of an organization. They explain how i-deals build upon larger frameworks of the law, collective agreements, and organizational practices, such that they always interact with the available regulations existing within organizations based on those higher-level rules and practices. As provocatively stated by the authors, signs of i-deals in organizations may be perceived as a failure of HRM, since the existing practices that are offered by the organization (and following law and collective agreements) do not suffice in the needs of employees for conditions that are important for them. However, this does not indicate a lack of reciprocity to i-deals by employees; Freese et al. explain how i-deals may have potential positive effects for organizations, teams, and individual employees and thus may contribute to more effective strategic HRM in organizations. Consequently, i-deals may actually contribute to organizational success, such that they complement existing rules and practices for employees and teams. However, there are also obvious negative effects, such as social comparison and fairness issues (Greenberg, Roberge, Ho, & Rousseau, 2004; Lai et al., 2009). Moreover, one of the less-discussed matters has been the mechanics and timing of i-deal negotiation and their subsequent management. For instance, there is very little knowledge on when i-deals are negotiated (e.g., just after getting a job or longer after one obtains a job), how they are managed (e.g., when a manager leaves the position, does an i-deal still apply?), or for how long i-deals are negotiated (e.g., for how long is a flexibility i-deal negotiated?). Similarly, little is known about the administrative challenges managers and employees face in making i-deals. With managers having increased spans of control, including dozens of subordinates, it is difficult for many managers to negotiate, manage, and have frequent chats with employees about their current or hoped-for i-deals. Finally, as previously recognized (Greenberg et al., 2004; Lai et al., 2009), organizations focused on equal treatment with respect to employees will need to adjust when using i-deals. How i-deals fit into the broader notion of equal treatment is itself a theoretical and practical concern.

The third part of the book focuses on the role of coworkers. First, Anand and Vidyarthi discuss in Chapter 7 the role of groups in i-deal negotiation processes. They zoomed in on the role of the leader, who is effectively responsible for the negotiation and management of i-deals in the workplace. The authors explain that employees with stronger relationships with their leaders *relative* to others tend to be more likely to successfully negotiate i-deals. They also demonstrate that i-deals are more likely to be negotiated when there is a leader who is open to the notion of i-deals and who is viewed as fair. Hence, for successful i-deal negotiation, the leader plays a crucial role, not only in the negotiation process, but also in communicating i-deal negotiation towards coworkers, and in this way preserving justice of i-deals. They also note that the same is true in organizations with cultures with an emphasis on respect for people and communal relations. Chapter 8 by Elise Marescaux and Sophie De Winne further disentangles the role of coworkers in this process. The authors empirically ascertained the roles of perceived equity and the perceived need of an i-deal, as assessed by coworkers. Fairness of an i-deal as perceived by coworkers was found to be predicated on the extent that the i-deal was seen as equitable as well as needed by the recipient. Moreover, while the first applied primarily to universalistic i-deals (involving resources of general value such as money), the latter pertained more to particularistic i-deals (such the opportunity to do a task that is personally enjoyable). For coworkers it is not only important that employees have earned the "right" to negotiate an i-deal in some fashion, but also that they have a problem that requires resolution. This resonates with the distinction made by Nauta and van de Ven regarding challenge and comfort i-deals. Challenge i-deals may be desired because employees perceive that they have some entitlement to an i-deal, while comfort i-deals may be negotiated by employees in order to solve some problem at work. Both approaches to distinguishing different types of i-deals are grounded in the notion of people differing in the needs and aims that motivate an i-deal and that coworkers will take these factors into account in assessing the i-deal's fairness (Greenberg et al., 2004; Lai et al., 2009).

An i-deals research agenda

A variety of new issues have emerged across these chapters. The first issue pertains to concept cleanup, that is, whether the empirical evidence to date actually operationalizes i-deals as they have been conceptualized and whether the empirical evidence is consistent with i-deal theory. The second matter is the psychosocial mechanisms influencing the creation of i-deals and their effects. The third involves the actual effort taken, if any, by either employer or employee to actually manage and shape the i-deal in the aftermath of its negotiation.

First, i-deals have been attributed to and even defined as the employer's effort to retain or attract valuable employees through individual bargaining (Huo, Luo, & Tam, 2014). Many i-deal researchers have started from this point of view. The implication is that i-deals are negotiated only by special employees, that is, those who the employer values most or those who believe themselves to somehow be distinct from their peers, thereby justifying special treatment. In contrast, i-deals may not emerge when employees are star performers, but also due to distinct individual needs not otherwise met by standard employment conditions. By broadening this, i-deals are no longer an investment in a highly valued employee but a general means of providing support for employee needs. This individualized treatment without a basis in the special value of a worker to the firm is at odds with traditional HRM systems, where standard treatment is the focus (Rousseau, 2005). Hence, future research should further investigate whether i-deals are primarily negotiated by valuable employees who have some entitlement to an i-deal (due to exceptional contributions to the organization), or that organizations also grant i-deals to employees who are not exceptional performers but do have some need for an individualized agreement. It may be the case that in some organizations, employees are granted i-deals because individualized arrangements enhance the perceptions of being treated as an individual rather than a resource.

The question also is whether organizations should treat only higher performing employees in an individual way, or that employees have a certain right to be treated as an individual, and whether i-deals can be regarded as an employee right. And how will organizations ensure individualized employment while maintaining justice in the organization (Greenberg et al., 2004)? This will be a prominent avenue for future research. For instance, research could focus on who are in the end able to negotiate i-deals, and whether it is the star performers or the privileged who actually obtain i-deals, or that i-deals are also used for other purposes, such as to repair damaged relationships or to accommodate employees who experience losses at work (Bal, Kooij, & De Jong, 2013). Hence, there is a need to understand the reasons why people start negotiating i-deals, as well as the motives organizations have for granting employees an i-deal.

Relatedly, presumptions have been made regarding the outcomes of i-deals, but only a few of these have actually been empirically examined. Research so far has primarily focused on employee attitudinal and behavioral outcomes, such as commitment, performance, and intention to continue working (Bal et al., 2012; Rosen et al., 2013). More fundamentally, benefits for both employees and organizations have been attributed to i-deals without empirical verification. Even though studies have shown significant correlations between i-deals and employee attitudes and behaviors, more in-depth study is needed regarding how and to which outcomes different types of i-deals are related. It is a question of whether some i-deals are negotiated with a certain outcome in mind for the employee and organization, whether outcomes have a more implicit character, or whether i-deals actually provide the benefits that theory and the parties to the negotiation presume they have. Given the social space in which i-deals operate and in which employee, employer, and coworkers maneuver, outcomes can also be realized across several levels. These include the employee (i.e., attitudinal or behavioral), the work group or team (e.g., team attitudes or behavior), and the organization (workforce performance or retention).

Research is needed to drill down into the mechanisms through which i-deals have an impact on outcomes. In the initial research on i-deals following the publication of Rousseau (2005), two specific mechanisms were the focus on both i-deal creation and impact. The first, social exchange theory, the initial grounding of i-deals theory (Rousseau et al., 2006), asserts that individuals tend to reciprocate contributions and favors with partners in a relationship, even when not otherwise required to do so (Blau, 1964). Employees with i-deals thus are expected to feel obligated to reciprocate through work efforts that ultimately benefit the employer (Rosen et al., 2013). The second, the pursuit of employee goals, was treated as both a motivator of customized employment arrangements and an explanation of its consequences (Latham & Locke, 1991). Goals are internal states through which individuals regulate their behavior in order to achieve a target. The goal of making one's job more interesting or personally motivating is reflected in theory regarding the role of i-deals as a means of redesigning one's job (Hornung, Rousseau, Glaser, Angerer, & Weigl, 2010). Recently, two other underlying mechanisms for i-deals have been empirically identified, the role of self-enhancement (Liu, Lee, Hui, Kwan, & Wu, 2013), and entitlement (Vidyarthi, Chaudhry, Anand, & Liden, 2014). Self-enhancement reflects concern with social comparison, particularly one's relative standing in relation to others, particularly within one's work group (Wood, 1996). Entitlement refers to a sense of being owed special treatment. Piff (2014) found that entitlement is associated with coming from a privileged social background (i.e., social economic status), as well as having a narcissistic personality. To date, research has treated these mechanisms in isolation with no study looking at their relative or potential confounded or competing effects.

Moderator effects are operating upon these theoretical mechanisms. To date, important moderators have been identified in terms of disposition (Liu et al., 2013), organizational norms (Bal et al., 2012), and societal factors (see Chapter 2 by Bal and Lub). Hence, a more complex picture of the dynamics underlying the effects of i-deals on outcomes emerges on the basis of the chapters in this book, and should receive more attention in future research.

Turning to operationalization and conceptualization of i-deals, it is imperative that i-deals are measured and investigated in line with their theoretical definition (cf. Rousseau, 2005; Rousseau et al., 2006), in particular, differentiating them from the shadier forms of individualized employment arrangements, preferential treatment, and corruption or rule breaking. Currently, measures of i-deals tend to Likert-scales combining both whether an i-deal has been negotiated, and how different its conditions are from other i-deals that colleagues negotiated (Hornung, Rousseau, & Glaser, 2008; Rosen et al., 2013). Perhaps more appropriate would be to first assess whether an i-deal has been agreed upon (yes/no dichotomy) and then to assess the nature and/or the distinctiveness of that deal from those of one's peers. Current i-deal measures contain an implicit assumption that i-deals are not dichotomous (yes or no) but rather psychologically experienced, leaving room for an assessment by the employee regarding the *extent* to which the employee has negotiated i-deals. Future research should investigate in-depth the validity of i-deal measures and develop further valid measures to fully understand i-deals in the workplace. It would also be valuable to investigate the degree of agreement between employee and employer (or supervisor) perspectives on whether a negotiated i-deal exists. Some discrepancy may be expected if an individual pursued an i-deal with a previous manager and continues to believe that it exists; however, the reality of an explicitly agreed-upon i-deal should be tested rather than merely assumed.

Finally, future research needs to investigate how i-deals are managed. I-deals break with more traditional standardized approaches towards human resource management (HRM). In departing from traditional personnel management approaches, organizations and managers must meet the challenge of promoting organizational justice in their use of individualized arrangements. Managers are likely to require training and development in order to effectively make and manage i-deals. Close interaction with HR departments can be crucial in maintaining and promoting successful i-deals in the workplace – and to capture learning regarding what works and what doesn't in particular organizational settings. To date there is no research on effective and ineffective ways to make and manage i-deals and none addressing how managers and organizations adjust to these new HR practices. As Chapter 6 details, i-deals have to fit within the larger context of law, collective agreements, and HR practices of an organization. I-deals need to comport with existing regulation and collective agreements. Further, we suspect that once employees have negotiated i-deals, little effort is undertaken on the part of many managers to oversee whether the deal realizes the benefits intended or to address unforeseen drawbacks. Attention to managing the i-deal in its aftermath can spell the difference between success or frustration (Huo et al., 2014). Both managers and employees are responsible for managing the agreements (Rousseau, 2006). And, last but not least, i-deals as exceptions may not remain viable or broadly beneficial in the long term. Yet little is known regarding how i-deals are evaluated over time and the ways in which they can be successfully ended while protecting the well-being of the parties involved.

This book and its authors have explicated important issues in the development and study of i-deals in the workplace. In doing so, it makes a case for the benefits and dilemmas of this increasingly prevalent employment practice. Notwithstanding the challenges they hold for both practice and future research, i-deals play a crucial and increasingly visible role in contemporary employment.

Note

1 Matthijs Bal, University of Bath, Bath, United Kingdom; Denise M. Rousseau, Carnegie Mellon University, Pittsburgh, USA.

References

Anand, S., Vidyarthi, P.R., Liden, R.C., & Rousseau, D.M. (2010). Good citizens in poor-quality relationships: Idiosyncratic deals as a substitute for relationship quality. *Academy of Management Journal, 53*(5), 970–988.

Bal, P.M., De Jong, S.B., Jansen, P.G.W., & Bakker, A.B. (2012). Motivating employees to work beyond retirement: A multi-level study of the role of i-deals and unit climate. *Journal of Management Studies, 49*, 306–331.

Bal, P.M., Kooij, D.T.A.M., & De Jong, S.B. (2013). How do developmental and accommodative HRM enhance employee engagement and commitment? The role of psychological contract and SOC-strategies. *Journal of Management Studies, 50*, 545–572.

Blau, P.M. (1964). *Exchange and power in social life*. New York: Transaction.

Greenberg, J., Roberge, M., Ho, V.T., & Rousseau, D.M. (2004). Fairness in idiosyncratic work arrangements: Justice as an i-deal. In J.J. Martocchio (Eds.), *Research in personnel and human resources management* (Vol. 23, pp. 1–34). Amsterdam: Elsevier.

Hornung, S., Rousseau, D.M., & Glaser, J. (2008). Creating flexible work arrangements through idiosyncratic deals. *Journal of Applied Psychology, 93*(3), 655–664.

Hornung, S., Rousseau, D.M., & Glaser, J. (2009). Why supervisors make idiosyncratic deals: Antecedents and outcomes of i-deals from a managerial perspective. *Journal of Managerial Psychology, 24*(8), 738–764.

Hornung, S., Rousseau, D.M., Glaser, J., Angerer, P., & Weigl, M. (2010). Beyond top-down and bottom-up work redesign: Customizing job content through idiosyncratic deals. *Journal of Organizational Behavior, 31*(2–3), 187–215.

Huo, W., Luo, J., & Tam, K.L. (2014). Idiosyncratic deals and good citizens in China: The role of traditionality for recipients and their coworkers. *The International Journal of Human Resource Management*, 1–21.

Lai, L., Rousseau, D.M., & Chang, K.T.T. (2009). Idiosyncratic deals: Coworkers as interested third parties. *Journal of Applied Psychology, 94*(2), 547–556.

Latham, G.P., & Locke, E.A. (1991). Self-regulation through goal setting. *Organizational Behavior and Human Decision Processes, 50*(2), 212–247.

Liu, J., Lee, C., Hui, C., Kwan, H.K., & Wu, L.-Z. (2013). Idiosyncratic deals and employee outcomes: The mediating roles of social exchange and self-enhancement and the moderating role of individualism. *Journal of Applied Psychology, 98*(5), 832–840.

Naumann, S.E., Minsky, B.D., & Sturman, M.C. (2002). The use of the concept "entitlement" in management literature: A historical review, synthesis, and discussion of compensation policy implications. *Human Resource Management Review, 12*(1), 145–166.

Piff, P.K. (2014). Wealth and the inflated self: Class entitlement and narcissism. *Personality and Social Psychology Bulletin, 40*, 34–43.

Rosen, C.C., Slater, D.J., Chang, C.-H., & Johnson, R.E. (2013). Let's make a deal: Development and validation of the ex post i-deals scale. *Journal of Management, 39*(3), 709–742.

Rousseau, D.M. (2005). *I-deals: Idiosyncratic deals employees bargain for themselves.* New York: M. E. Sharpe.

Rousseau, D.M., Ho, V.T., & Greenberg, J. (2006). I-deals: Idiosyncratic terms in employment relationships. *Academy of Management Review, 31,* 977–994.

Vidyarthi, P.R., Chaudhry, A., Anand, S., & Liden, R.C. (2014). Flexibility i-deals: How much is ideal? *Journal of Managerial Psychology, 29*(3), 246–265.

Wood, J.V. (1996). What is social comparison and how should we study it? *Personality and Social Psychology Bulletin, 22,* 520–537.

INDEX

abstract i-deals 27–8
aggressiveness 99
alignment 74–5

benefits of i-deals 2, 10, 37, 54–5, 79–80, 82–3, 94

career 10–11, 16, 27, 65–72, 80, 124; development 67, 100, 102; growth 92
challenge i-deals 68–9
collectivistic 12, 100
comfort i-deals 68–9
commitment 9, 24, 84, 101, 127
conceptualization 4, 20, 92–3, 123, 128
content of i-deals 27–8, 109, 111, 113, 117
costs of i-deals 54–5, 80–1
coworker acceptance 20, 123
customization 1, 15, 76, 78, 96

damaged relationships 24–35
development i-deals 10, 28, 75, 79, 84
dialogue coaching 70
differentiation 74–7, 86, 101
dignity 12–18
distributive justice 58, 108–10, 113, 115

employability 13, 70, 80, 85, 92
entitlement 2, 20, 59, 125, 127
equality 66, 109
equity 26, 54, 107–21
equity theory 110
explicit negotiation 53–4

factor analyses 114
fairness 9, 20, 26, 54, 80, 82; leader fairness 96–7
favouritism 2, 9, 54–5, 123
financial i-deals 3, 75, 108, 111, 118
flexibility i-deals 10, 69, 75, 83, 110; work location 111; work schedules 2, 111

gender 112
goals 73, 127

heterogeneity 2, 58, 101
high commitment HRM 19
history of i-deals 31
human capital theory 79
human dignity *see* dignity

individualism 9, 12, 59, 124
initiation 28–9
intention to continue working 127

job content 67, 80, 111
job crafting 4, 11
job design 4, 92
justice 26, 58–9, 66, 108

leaders 77, 87, 93; openness 95–6
line managers 87
LMX 15, 25, 93, 123
LMX differentiation 94–5

management of i-deals 69–70, 85–7, 124, 128
Matthew Effect 13, 19, 69, 84, 86–7
measurement of i-deals 59–60
mutual benefits 54–5

need 107–21
neoliberalism 12–20
norm of reciprocity 3, 11

Occupy Wall Street 17
organizational climate 78, 81
organizational culture 86, 98–9

particularistic resources 27–8, 31, 111
person-environment fit 75, 77
power 1, 13, 15, 27, 84–5
proactivity 16, 20, 29, 37, 95
procedural justice 58, 87, 119
psychological contract 3–4, 10, 14, 24, 28–30, 53, 57, 76
psychologicalization 10

regression analyses 115–16
relationship repair 25, 31–2; attributional, social equilibrium, and structural processes 25
relative LMX 94–5
requests for i-deals 78
research designs 52, 60–1
resource-based view 79

respect for people 99
retirement age 67, 80

scope 2, 37, 55
secondary elastics 78, 80
self-enhancement theory 3
social comparison 58, 60, 94, 101, 127
social exchange theory 3, 11, 62, 127
social justice 20
social role theory 112–13
special needs i-deals 75, 82
standardization 81, 85–6
strategic differentiation 77
strategic HRM 73–91
synergy 74

talents 79–80, 83
tangible i-deals 27
team level 82–3
team orientation 100
team potency 102–3
timing 30, 60, 125
transaction costs 81, 85

unfairness *see* fairness
uniqueness 76, 82, 84
universal resources 27–8, 111

we-deal 76–7
win-win deals 55, 108
work-group attributes 98